CANADIAN CHALLENGES

Don Quinlan
Series Editor

Aboriginal Peoples Building for the Future

Kevin Reed

CONTENTS

All terms appearing in boldfaced type in the text are defined in the Glossary that appears on page 96.

FOCUS

This section will help you understand
- a. why it is important to study Aboriginal peoples' perspective
- b. the challenges involved in learning about Aboriginal peoples.

> We dream about...a time when we can use our own political judgment, our own free will to shape our destinies and control our own affairs.
> —Ovide Mercredi, past Grand Chief of the Assembly of First Nations.

Changing Perspectives

Ask yourself what you know about Aboriginal peoples in Canada today. You may know a little about some early Aboriginal cultures. You've probably learned about Aboriginal peoples when the first Europeans arrived, their involvement with the fur trade, and their relations with early French, British, and Canadian governments. What about the history of Aboriginal peoples since 1900? In the past, most Canadian history books included very little about Aboriginal peoples in the 20th century. In fact,

people may have concluded that Aboriginal cultures disappeared from Canada sometime before 1900.

Today, we know that Aboriginal peoples are an important part of Canadian history. We realize that their rights and contributions must be recognized. It is also becoming clear that the issues facing Aboriginal peoples affect all Canadians. The study of Aboriginal history, however, presents some unique challenges.

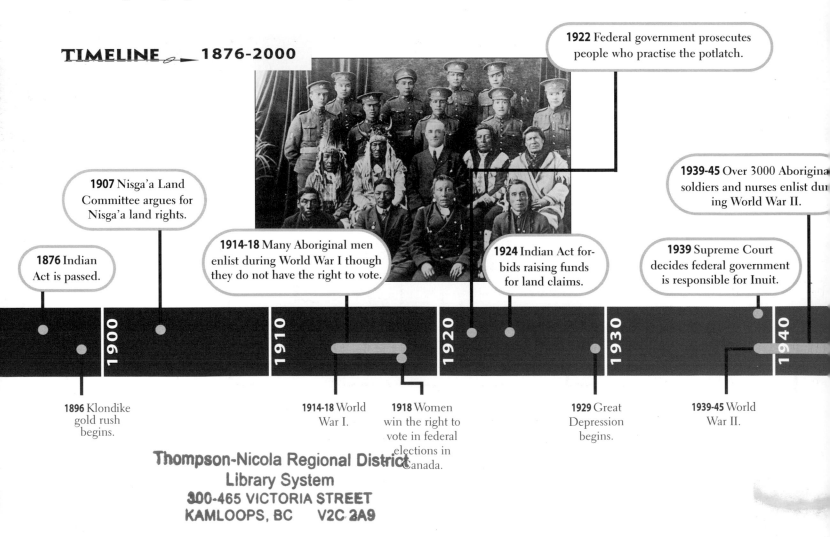

TIMELINE 1876-2000

1922 Federal government prosecutes people who practise the potlatch.

1939-45 Over 3000 Aboriginal soldiers and nurses enlist during World War II.

1907 Nisga'a Land Committee argues for Nisga'a land rights.

1876 Indian Act is passed.

1914-18 Many Aboriginal men enlist during World War I though they do not have the right to vote.

1924 Indian Act forbids raising funds for land claims.

1939 Supreme Court decides federal government is responsible for Inuit.

1896 Klondike gold rush begins.

1914-18 World War I.

1918 Women win the right to vote in federal elections in Canada.

1929 Great Depression begins.

1939-45 World War II.

1900 · 1910 · 1920 · 1930 · 1940

Biases and New Directions

History books reflect the ideas and interests of those who write them. Like most people, historians tend to see the world in light of their own backgrounds and experiences. For example, Canadian historians often consider industrialization and immigration to be two of the most important changes in Canada during the 20th century. In their study, however, they may overlook the effect those changes had on Aboriginal peoples and their lives. This is a form of **bias** called ethnocentrism. Ethnocentrism means viewing the world only in terms of our own ethnic group or culture. As a result, we may either ignore other groups or misunderstand and have a distorted view of them. This bias is very common and difficult to spot in our own thinking.

As you read through this book and others, keep your eyes open for historical and current examples of ethnocentrism. Sometimes ethnocentrism can result in **stereotypical** and even racist views of Aboriginal peoples. Think about this as you examine the cartoon and photographs on the next page.

Before 1900 Aboriginal peoples were a large part of the population in many parts of Canada and they dealt directly with governments and other groups. During the 20th century, Aboriginal peoples have become a minority within Canadian society. They have often been ignored and their experiences have been considered unimportant. In other words, they have been marginalized—pushed to the edge or margin of Canadian society and history.

Today, many more historians are focusing on **social history**. They are studying the daily lives of all types of people. They are also recognizing the importance of all groups, large or small, and considering what we can learn from their experiences, cultures, and achievements.

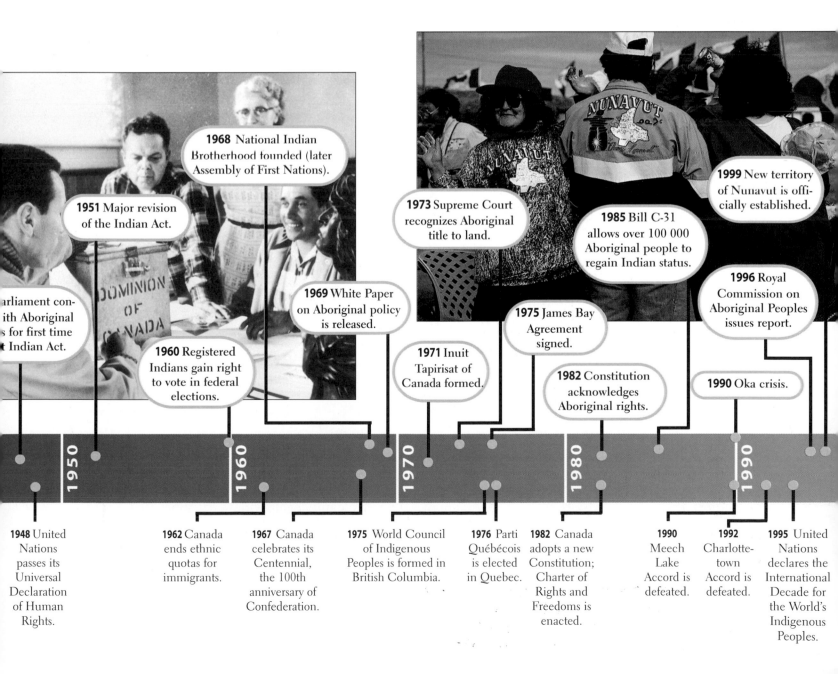

1968 National Indian Brotherhood founded (later Assembly of First Nations).

1951 Major revision of the Indian Act.

arliament con-
ith Aboriginal
s for first time
Indian Act.

1969 White Paper on Aboriginal policy is released.

1960 Registered Indians gain right to vote in federal elections.

1973 Supreme Court recognizes Aboriginal title to land.

1985 Bill C-31 allows over 100 000 Aboriginal people to regain Indian status.

1999 New territory of Nunavut is officially established.

1996 Royal Commission on Aboriginal Peoples issues report.

1975 James Bay Agreement signed.

1971 Inuit Tapirisat of Canada formed.

1982 Constitution acknowledges Aboriginal rights.

1990 Oka crisis.

1950   1960   1970   1980   1990

1948 United Nations passes its Universal Declaration of Human Rights.

1962 Canada ends ethnic quotas for immigrants.

1967 Canada celebrates its Centennial, the 100th anniversary of Confederation.

1975 World Council of Indigenous Peoples is formed in British Columbia.

1976 Parti Québécois is elected in Quebec.

1982 Canada adopts a new Constitution; Charter of Rights and Freedoms is enacted.

1990 Meech Lake Accord is defeated.

1992 Charlotte-town Accord is defeated.

1995 United Nations declares the International Decade for the World's Indigenous Peoples.

CaseStudy

EXAMINING IMAGES PAST AND PRESENT

Figure 1-2   Even the types of pictures presented in books and the media can cause bias. Analyse these pictures and describe the image of Aboriginal people each one creates.

Figure 1-1 A cartoon from *The Canadian West*, 1906. Who has the cartoonist included in this cartoon? Who is excluded? What is the cartoon's intended meaning? What other meanings might it have?

Sources of Aboriginal History

Traditionally, historians have relied on written documents. Until recently, however, Aboriginal peoples had mainly oral cultures. They passed on their laws, history, and sacred traditions through stories, songs, events retold, **genealogies**, and place names that did not need to be written down. As a result, they produced few written documents. In fact, most documents which refer to Aboriginal people were written by non-Aboriginal people. Since those writers may not have understood historical events as Aboriginal peoples did, the documents may be unintentionally or even intentionally biased. Also, non-Aboriginal people often have difficulty accepting oral evidence, especially if it relates to events dating back several generations.

Recently, historians and official Canadian bodies such as the Supreme Court of Canada have accepted Aboriginal oral traditions as "real" historical and legal evidence. Aboriginal peoples are also actively working to rediscover aspects of their history. Many are recording the stories and knowledge they recover in different mediums so that this information is not forgotten.

Primary Source
WAMPUM AND ORAL HISTORY

The following oral history describes the relationship between the Haudenosaunee (Iroquois) Confederacy and Europeans as symbolized in the Two-row Wampum Belt, an important source of history for members of the Confederacy.

When your ancestors came to our shores, after living with them for a few years, observing them, our ancestors came to the conclusion that we could not live together in the same way inside the circle…So our leaders at that time, along with your leaders, sat down for many years to try to work out a solution. This is what they come up with. We call it Gus-Wen-Tah, or the Two-row Wampum Belt. It is on a bed of white wampum, which symbolizes the purity of the agreement. There are two rows of purple, and those two rows have the spirit of our ancestors; those two rows never come together in that belt, and it is easy to see what that means. It means that we have two different paths, two different people.

The agreement was made that your road will have your vessel, your people, your politics, your government, your way of life, your religion, your beliefs—they are all in there. The same goes for ours…They said there will be three beads of wampum separating the two, and they will symbolize peace, friendship, and respect.

—*Quoted in the Report of the Royal Commission on Aboriginal Peoples, Vol. 1, p. 103.*

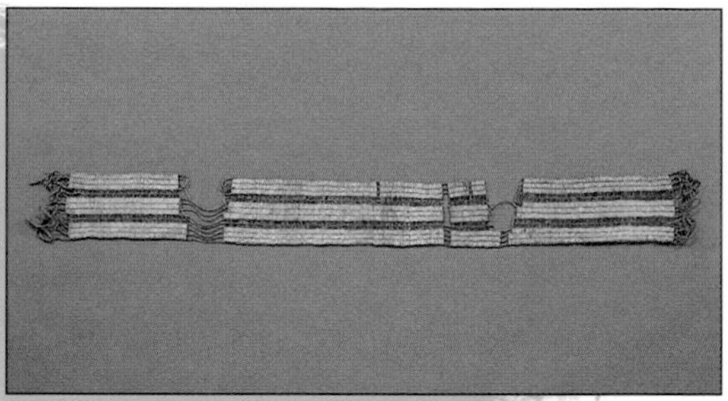

Figure 1-3 The Two-row Wampum Belt of the Haudenosaunee (Iroquois) Confederacy. Wampum, tiny beads made from sea shells, was a way for the Haudenosaunee First Nations to record their history and sacred agreements. The designs and colours used in each belt held a particular message. These messages were memorized by wampum keepers, or historians. When a pact was made the terms were recorded in the design of the belt.

Aboriginal History in this Book

In this book we will focus mainly on the frequently neglected story of Aboriginal peoples from Confederation to the present. We will examine how governments in Canada tried to control Aboriginal peoples and to **assimilate** or absorb them into Canadian society. We will also study how Aboriginal peoples tried to control and improve their own lives. We aim to highlight their achievements and let you hear *their* voices on major events and issues. Like all people, Aboriginal peoples have not always been successful in achieving their goals and they still face many challenges. They have, however, consistently argued for their rights and for control over the lands they consider rightfully theirs.

Figure 1-4 Some West Coast First Nations recorded their oral histories in the designs of totem poles, crests and blankets. These oral histories describe the most important laws, history, traditions, and traditional territory of a clan. Their importance is underlined by the fact that they are repeated, performed, and authenticated at important feasts. This Gitksan totem pole was raised in 1973.

RECONNECT

1. Explain marginalization, ethnocentrism, and assimilate in your own words.

2. Why do you think some people in Canada have difficulty accepting oral history?

Who Are the Aboriginal Peoples of Canada?

FOCUS

This section will help you understand
- a. the diversity of Aboriginal peoples and cultures in Canada
- b. the meanings of the terms Status or Registered Indian, Métis, and Inuit.

The Diversity of Aboriginal Peoples

Aboriginal peoples were the first inhabitants of what is now Canada. When Europeans arrived, Aboriginal peoples had been living on the lands for thousands of years. They spoke more than 50 languages and had a rich diversity of **cultures**. Their cultures reflected close ties with their lands and environments. Across the continent, the groups displayed a dazzling variety in their sacred rituals, foods, clothing, art, tools, governments, social organizations, and patterns of everyday life. The Haida on the West Coast, for example, had a culture very distinct from the Ojibwa or the Mi'kmaq in the east.

Many Aboriginal groups were hunters and gatherers. These groups lived migratory lives before the 20th century. That is, they moved around specific territories according to the seasons, hunting and gathering food for their own needs. They spent most of the year living in family groups or **clans** and gathered into larger bands only at special times in the year. The Siksika (Blackfoot), for example, followed the buffalo which was the main source of their livelihood and an important symbol in their culture. They gathered into larger, highly organized groups for a major hunt at specific times in the year. Many groups in the Subarctic focused on the winter caribou hunt and gathered resources from the sea and rivers in the other months.

Other groups, particularly on the West Coast and in the Eastern Woodlands, lived in more permanent communities. The warmer climate on the West Coast allowed the people to get food from the sea year round. Peoples of the Eastern Woodlands developed agriculture and grew crops in settled communities.

Figure 2-1 Aboriginal peoples on the West Coast lived in settled villages such as this one, with large homes made from cedar planks and decorated with the crests and totems of the families or clans.

Many groups traded regularly with one another and sometimes formed political **alliances**. The Iroquois Confederacy or League of Haudenosaunee (People of the Longhouse) resulted from a peace treaty among five, and later six, First Nations south of the Great Lakes. The Confederacy had an elaborate constitution called the Great Law of Peace which governed relations among the member nations. The Blackfoot Confederacy on the Prairies included the Siksika (the Blackfoot), the Blood, and the Peigan.

Today, many Aboriginal people and other Canadians refer to these early Aboriginal groups as First Nations. This reflects the view that they were independent, self-governing societies before the arrival of Europeans. They had their own governments, laws, and social systems. They educated their children in their own ways and practised their own sacred rituals.

MapStudy — FIRST NATIONS AT THE TIME OF CONTACT

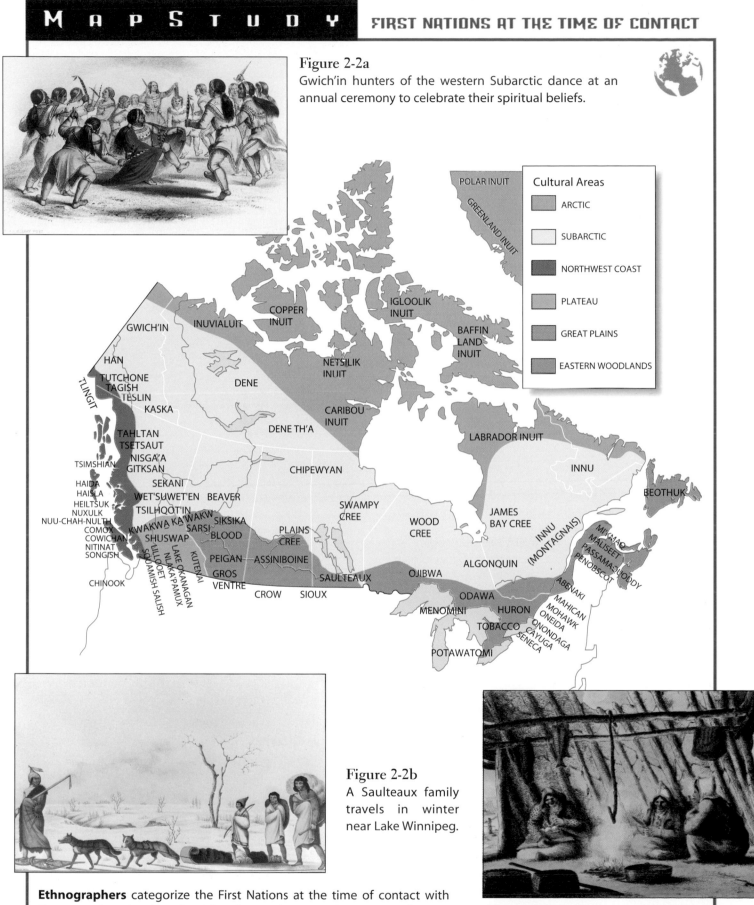

Figure 2-2a
Gwich'in hunters of the western Subarctic dance at an annual ceremony to celebrate their spiritual beliefs.

Cultural Areas
- ARCTIC
- SUBARCTIC
- NORTHWEST COAST
- PLATEAU
- GREAT PLAINS
- EASTERN WOODLANDS

Figure 2-2b
A Saulteaux family travels in winter near Lake Winnipeg.

Figure 2-2c Mi'kmaq women gather and work in a wigwam on the East Coast.

Ethnographers categorize the First Nations at the time of contact with Europeans into the six major cultural areas shown on the map. Use the map to identify the cultural group and specific First Nations who lived in your part of Canada around 1500. Do these First Nations still live in your area?

Contact and Change

Contact with Europeans had a profound impact on Aboriginal peoples and their cultures. Diseases such as smallpox wiped out a large part of the original population. The loss in population weakened Aboriginal communities and undermined their cultures.

As well, competition for furs due to government policies created a new element of instability in relations among Aboriginal peoples. While there were conflicts before the Europeans arrived, they were not generally widespread or destructive. The introduction of muskets and rifles increased the competition and the bloodiness of some conflicts. Aboriginal peoples also became involved in wars between European nations battling for control over North America.

The ever increasing pressure of European and Canadian settlement and government policies under the Indian Act forced some Aboriginal peoples out of their traditional territories. As the story in this book will tell, their numbers were drastically reduced, their lives were disrupted, traditions were lost, and governments attempted to marginalize them, or absorb them into Canadian society. Throughout this period, they continually struggled to assert their rights. Today Aboriginal peoples are also working to redefine their identities and recover aspects of their traditions.

Aboriginal Peoples Today

Today, the federal government divides Aboriginal peoples into four main groups: Registered or Status Indians, Non-Registered or Non-Status Indians, Métis and Inuit. These legal terms do not necessarily refer to the amount of "Aboriginal blood" a person has, or to cultural or social characteristics. Rather, they rely on a combination of historical factors such as treaties, marriage, and biological descent.

In common with current usage, this book uses the following terms:

▶ Aboriginal peoples refers to First Nations people, Métis and Inuit.
▶ First Nations refers to Aboriginal peoples before European contact or to legally defined Indian bands and Registered Indians today.
▶ Indian is only used to refer to First Nations people when they are discussed in the context of government regulations such as the Indian Act or in quotations.
▶ Métis and Inuit are used in their legal sense on page 9.

Primary Source

"We must be the ones who determine who is and who is not a member of our community, based on criteria accepted by our people. A good example is the approach taken by the Dene people in the North. For them, membership requires family connection, a knowledge of Dene culture and language, and a commitment to the good of the people. For them, identity is not based on race but on culture and family; it reflects Dene values."

—Ovide Mercredi, quoted in *In the Rapids: Navigating the Future of First Nations* (Toronto: Viking, Penguin Books Canada Ltd., 1993), p. 88.

CONNECTIONS

Some First Nations are returning to their traditional names rather than those used by European explorers.

Original or New Name	Traditional European/Canadian Name
Inuit—means "the people" in Inuktituk (the Inuit language).	Eskimo—possibly an Algonkian term meaning "raw meat eaters."
Siksika—means "black foot."	Blackfoot—a direct translation from the language of the Siksika into English.
Kwakwa̱ ka̱' wakw—means "those who speak Kwak'wala."	Kwakiutl—a name which means "on the other side of the river"—and refers to only one of the groups which speak Kwak'wala.
Nuu-chah-nulth—means "all along the mountains."	Nootka—dates from the arrival of Captain Cook but its meaning is unclear.
Innu—means "the people."	Montagnais—derives from the French word for "mountain" and Naskapi—origin unknown.

Legal Terms Describing Aboriginal Peoples in Canada

Registered or Status Indians

First Nations peoples whose ancestors signed treaties with the federal government or were recognized by the government as belonging to a First Nations community. Indian status can be gained by birth, marriage, or adoption. All Status Indians are registered with the federal government.

Most Status Indians also belong to an Indian band. An Indian band is a group of Indians for whom the government holds common lands called a reserve. There are about 600 Indian bands in Canada and 2300 reserves. Status Indians who have band membership may or may not live on reserves.

Status Indians are governed by the rules of the Indian Act. They receive free post-secondary education, pay no income taxes on income earned on reserves, do not pay provincial sales taxes for goods bought on reserves, have special hunting and fishing rights, are entitled to housing on a reserve if they are band members, and may emigrate easily to the United States.

Métis

People of mixed heritage (First Nations or Inuit and European) who identify with the traditional Métis culture or whose ancestors received payments called scrip in recognition of land rights. Although the federal government acknowledged the treaty and Aboriginal rights of the Métis in the 1870s, it did not keep complete records of this popu-

lation until 1981. The Métis do not have the rights of Status Indians at this time, although they are recognized as a separate Aboriginal people in the Canadian Constitution.

Inuit

Aboriginal peoples who traditionally live in the Arctic or in northern Quebec and Labrador. The rules governing who is an Inuk are complicated. For example, in the 1975 James Bay Agreement, an Inuk (a single Inuit person) was defined as someone who is considered an Inuk by a community, or has one-quarter Inuit blood, or possesses a "disc" number from the original census of the Inuit by the Canadian government. In 1939, the federal government was forced by the courts to take full responsibility for the Inuit. Like Status Indians, the Inuit receive special rights from the government although they are not covered by the Indian Act.

Non-Registered or Non-Status Indians

First Nations people whose ancestors were never identified as Indians by the government or who lost their status. The Innu who live in Labrador, for example, did not receive Indian status when Newfoundland entered Confederation in 1949. Non-Status Indians are not eligible for the benefits Status Indians receive and are not subject to the Indian Act.

These categories used by the federal government do not reflect the variety of Aboriginal peoples living in Canada today. Aboriginal peoples today speak many different languages and have a wide variety of cultural traditions. They live in different areas across the country, some in cities and some on reserves. Despite their differences, many share a strong desire to reclaim important parts of their heritage. They want to define their cultural identities in the present and for the future.

Figure 2-3 Aboriginal language teacher Annie Boulanger gives a lesson to a student. There are 50 Aboriginal languages in Canada, many of which are in danger of disappearing.

Figure 2-4 Powwow in Mission B.C. Originally "powwow" referred to celebrations held to begin a hunt or council gathering. Today, Aboriginal peoples from many different places come together at powwows to celebrate their traditional dances and songs and to renew ties with one another.

RECONNECT

1. Briefly explain the terms, Métis, Inuit, Registered or Status Indian, Non-Registered or Non-Status Indian, and Aboriginal peoples.

2. Why do you think Aboriginal peoples are reclaiming their traditional names?

Aboriginal World View

FOCUS

This section will help you understand
a. how Aboriginal people have traditionally viewed the universe
b. how this world view still has value and influence today.

From Past to Present

Most Aboriginal people today live in modern ways but many are rediscovering and preserving aspects of their traditional cultures and making them part of their daily lives. They feel that their traditional stories, rituals, and spiritual beliefs are important parts of who they are and have value in their modern lives.

Aboriginal peoples have different beliefs. Traditionally, however, they have shared some common views about the nature of the world and the place of humans in it. These common beliefs, or world view, affected how Aboriginal peoples saw events in the world and how they behaved and interacted. Some of these common beliefs include:

▶ everything in the world, both living and non-living, is connected,
▶ unseen spiritual powers exist and affect all things,
▶ everything in the world constantly changes in recurring cycles, and
▶ humans need to be in harmony with each other and with nature.

Humans and Nature

For some Aboriginal peoples, humans are one with nature or Creation. They are not separate from it and do not have a special or dominant place in it. Therefore, all people have a responsibility to respect other humans, animals, birds, plants, and inanimate objects—or in the words of the great Oglala Sioux spiritual elder Black Elk, the two-leggeds, four-leggeds, wingeds, and standing people (plants). Everything in the world, living or non-living, has a spirit and should be honoured. Even human-made objects have a spirit.

Many Aboriginal creation and recreation stories reflect this relationship between humans and the natural world. In many of these stories, animals co-operate in the creation of the world and the first peoples. For example, in a recreation story in the Ojibwa tradition, the earth was once covered with water in a great flood. Several water animals and birds (the beaver, marten, fisher and loon) tried to bring some mud to the surface of the water.

Primary Source

We know that we are related and are one with all things of the heavens and the earth, and we know that all the things that move are a people as we. We all wish to live and increase in a holy manner ... May we be continually aware of this relationship which exists between the four-leggeds, the two-leggeds, and the wingeds. May we all rejoice and live in peace!

—Black Elk, an Oglala Sioux holy man, quoted in *The Sacred Pipe: Black Elk's Account of the Seven Sacred Rites of the Oglala Sioux,* ed. Joseph Epes Brown (Norman: University of Oklahoma Press, 1953), p. 97.

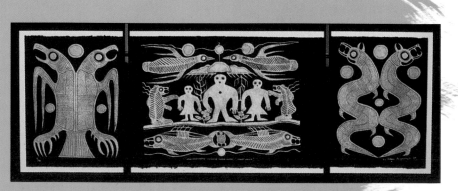

Figure 3-1 Some Aboriginal peoples believe in the interdependence of all creatures who live in the sky, on earth, and in the water. This print, *Skyworld, Middle World and Underworld* is by Ahmoo Angeconeb from the Lac Seul First Nation.

Figure 3-2 In *Birth of the Earth* by Onondaga artist Arnold Jacobs, a divine woman falls from the sky and with the help of the animals creates the earth. This painting reflects the belief that humans are not separate from nature.

Eventually, a muskrat succeeded. Sky Woman then spread the mud on the back of a turtle and created Turtle Island, the Ojibwa name for North America. In Haida legend, it is the Raven, alone in the world, who coaxes the original people out from a clamshell on a beach. The original Haida thus came from the sea, which has remained a key element in their livelihood and culture.

Harmony and Balance

For many Aboriginal peoples, everything in creation follows a cycle of change. The seasons change regularly, and animals and plants have yearly cycles of migration and birth. Human life also follows a cycle. Humans are born, mature, and die and then pass on into the spirit world. The circle is a central symbol in many Aboriginal cultures, reflecting these cycles. The circle also represents the connection of all things.

Despite the changing world, humans must live in harmony with the natural order. Each culture has its own songs, rituals, ceremonies and dances to keep in

Primary Source

ANIMALS IN OJIBWA LEGENDS

In Ojibwa legends, animals not only helped create the Earth, they also helped the original humans. Ojibwa legends say that bears played a particularly important part in the survival of the first humans.

> For all their needs the spirit woman and her children depended on the care and goodwill of the animals. The bears, wolves, foxes, deer and beaver brought food and drink; the squirrels, weasels, racoons, and cats offered toys and games; the robins, sparrows, chickadees, and loons sang and danced in the air; the butterflies, bees, and dragonflies made the children smile… The bear, fearing the death of the infants, offered himself that they might live.

> With the bear's sweet flesh, the infants survived. The death of the bear encompassed life for the new beings. Thereafter, the other animals sacrificed their lives for the good of men. When the infants grew to manhood and womanhood, they bore a special love for the bear and honoured him in their ceremonies. In gratitude and fondness they dedicated a prayer to the other animals, "I had need." Men and women survive and live because of the death of their elder brothers.

—Basil Johnston, *Ojibway Heritage: The Ceremonies, Rituals, Songs, Dances, Prayers, and Legends of the Ojibway* (Toronto: McClelland and Stewart Inc., 1976), p. 16.

Figure 3-3 The bear is a sacred animal in Ojibwa legends. This painting is called *Bear Feeding* by Blake Debassige. Debassige's artwork interprets the Ojibwa way of life.

touch with the spiritual world and to honour the spirits. Aboriginal people try to consider the effect of their actions seven generations into the future. They are also taught to honour and respect the animals they hunt. If the proper respect for animals was not shown, Aboriginal people believed they would not respond to a hunter's request for "good hunting." To the Cree, for example, this means not pointing at an animal or walking in its tracks when hunting it. As well, the hunters are restrained in their celebration of the kill. They display the animal's carcass respectfully in their home and dispose of the bones with care. The Cree, like many other First Nations, also express a strong belief in their responsibility to protect and preserve the land. All people are connected to the spirit of the land. It provides life, knowledge, healing, and a connection to all Creation.

Figure 3-4   Cree hunters show great respect for the animals they hunt and dispose of the bones with care. A set of caribou horns sits on a raised platform near a hunting camp. The skulls of smaller animals are also placed there to show respect.

CultureLink

TRADITIONAL VALUES OF THE OJIBWA (ANISHINABE) PEOPLE

According to the Sacred Teachings of the Midewiwin Spiritual Way, the Ojibwa should practise the Seven Gifts of the Grandfathers. These gifts describe basic values of the Ojibwa people.

1. To cherish knowledge is to know **wisdom**.
2. To know **love** is to know peace.
3. To honour all of creation is to have **respect**.
4. **Bravery** is to face the foe with integrity.
5. **Honesty** is facing a situation is to be brave.
6. **Humility** is to know yourself as a sacred part of creation.
7. **Truth** is to know all these things.

Source: James Dumont quoted in Royal Commission on Aboriginal Peoples, *(Ottawa: Minister of Supply Services, 1993), p. 45.*

Traditional Knowledge Today

In the Northwest Territories, regulations require government officials to recognize the traditional knowledge that Aboriginal peoples have about animals and the land. When decisions are made about resource development and wildlife management, government officials must consult with Aboriginal peoples about the possible impact on the natural environment.

In other cases, First Nations have not been consulted about development projects and are actively opposing them. The Cree Nation, for example, has opposed any expansion or further development by Hydro-Québec in the North for many years. They believe the original James Bay project caused massive destruction to the environment. They are concerned about further damage and they want their claims to the lands recognized.

In many ways, the Aboriginal view reflects current concerns about **ecology** and the environment. For example, many scientists acknowledge that the traditional Inuit classification of animals in the North will help advance the understanding of Arctic **ecosystems**. The views of scientists and Aboriginal peoples do not always agree, however. Scientists and Inuit clash over the hunting of some whale species in the North, which scientists consider endangered.

CROSSFIRE

Read the following reactions to proposed hydro development projects in northern Quebec.

My people are determined to stand up against any project having to do with the destruction of the land, water and other resources that have sustained us as a people since time immemorial… No amount of money in the world can replace the type of destruction that took place at La Grande, and this is not going to happen here… Lake Bienville is a sacred area. It is the heart of the land. Its huge water area contains all kinds of fish that has sustained the Eeyouch (Cree people). It is the central calving ground for the inland caribou. Birds and animals of all kinds have used and continue to use this area as a sanctuary. It just cannot be touched by man. Any alteration to it will bring bad luck to the perpetrator because it is a sacred area.

—Chief Matthew Mukash, leader of the Cree community of Great Whale River, *Canada News Wire*, July 31, 1997 www.newswire.ca

"Hydro-Québec is not a diviner, but we still have a responsibility to meet the needs of our customers." In its $400-million feasibility study [for the proposed Great Whale project], Hydro-Québec argued that the power was needed to fulfill Quebec's rising energy needs after the year 2000, largely driven by demand from New England. It also argued that the project would create 66 700 direct and indirect jobs over 10 years, generating $10.7 million in annual spinoffs for the region. Native people, for their part, would receive some $130 million in compensation.

—Editorial published in *The Globe and Mail*, Nov. 22, 1994, p. A22.

The Crees' position is clear. The Crees' position is that diversion projects are unacceptable. We want to look at alternatives to any projects that are announced. We would certainly want a public debate on an energy policy. We would want it to look at more than the economics of projects. It should examine the social, environmental and cultural impacts. We are still concerned about the environmental audit to be done on the past impacts.

—Cree Grand Chief Matthew Coon Come in an interview with *The Nation*, December 5, 1997.

RECONNECT

1. Write a paragraph explaining your reactions to the Aboriginal world view. Be sure to discuss each of the four common beliefs mentioned on page 10.

2. How is the Aboriginal world view influencing environmental issues today?

FOCUS

This section will help you understand
  a. the types of ceremonies and rituals practised by Aboriginal peoples
  b. the purposes of ceremonies and rituals and their importance for Aboriginal peoples today.

From Traditional to Modern

Aboriginal peoples in Canada practised a wide variety of ceremonies and **rituals** when Europeans first arrived hundreds of years ago. Until the mid-20th century, European missionaries, Christian converts, and the federal government tried to stop these Aboriginal practices. Many Aboriginal people were converted to Christianity and lost their traditional beliefs. Today, however, various rituals and ceremonies are being practised openly again. In fact, Aboriginal people see these practices as a way to revitalize their communities. They have adapted many traditional rituals to deal with the needs and concerns in their present communities. Some Aboriginal people today combine both Christian and Aboriginal practices.

Ceremonies and rituals were held for many different purposes, some spiritual and some social. Ceremonies connected people to the spirit world and to each other. Often personal experiences such as **vision quests** were combined with public ceremonies such as dances. Various ceremonies and rituals were held for healing and purifying the spirit, for honour-ing animal spirits and offering thanksgiving, or for celebrating important seasonal, social, or family events.

Each First Nation had its own particular practices and variations. For example, on the West Coast during the winter months, First Nations performed sacred dance cycles and held **potlatches** to confirm titles on important members of the community or clan. Amid dancing, feasting, and gift-giving, chiefs were named, marriages celebrated, or children adopted.

Purification Ceremonies and Rituals

Aboriginal ceremonies or gatherings often begin with the burning of a sacred product, such as sweet grass, tobacco, cedar, sage or red willow bark. The Peigan, for example, burn sweet grass as a personal blessing

EyeWitness

A Living Culture

There is some criticism that contemporary potlatches are not like they were "in the old days." How could they be? The world we live in today is vastly different from that in which our grandparents lived. A typical potlatch is now completed in one day, rather than the several days required in earlier times... Today, we write out names and dances, because there are no longer recordkeepers as there were in the old days who could keep all this information in their minds. We videotape potlatches these days, something unheard of in our grandparents' time. If a culture is alive, it does not remain static. Ours is definitely alive and changes as the times require.

—Gloria Cranmer Webster, "From Colonization to Repatriation" in *Indigena: Contemporary Native Perspectives*, eds. Gerald McMaster and Lee-Ann Martin (Vancouver: Douglas & McIntyre and Canadian Museum of Civilization, 1992), p. 36.

Figure 4-1 Participants at the Qatuwas Festival gather in front of the U'Mista Cultural Centre at Alert Bay, B.C. to welcome the canoes returning to shore. The Qatuwas Festival is an annual festival.

during ceremonies and use sage to purify the mind and body. People may *smudge* themselves by drawing the smoke over their bodies. In this way, the burning acts as an offering to the spirits and the smoke cleanses the body and mind.

Many Aboriginal peoples in North America also use sweat lodge ceremonies for purification. A sweat lodge is a constructed dome made of saplings. This framework is then covered with animal skins, blankets or tarpaulins, and usually cedar boughs to form a small, sealed and dark place. Hot stones are brought into a small pit at the centre of the lodge and water is poured over the stones to produce steam. The steam purifies the mind and body. There are often rounds of prayers and sometimes a sacred pipe is shared. The ceremony reconnects people with themselves, the world, each other, and all creation. Because of its spiritual significance, an elder or shaman (spiritual leader) usually leads the sweat lodge ceremony.

Vision Quests

A vision quest is a way to make a powerful and personal connection with the spirit world. Often, a person fasts and prays while searching for a vision of a guiding spirit. Aboriginal people may undertake a vision quest during a child's illness, during a time of personal doubt and uncertainty, or at puberty.

Figure 4-2   Shaman Russell Willier prepares for a pipe ceremony. Some First Nations use the sacred pipe in healing ceremonies, to open important meetings, and to signify important events such as hunts. Agreements solemnized by the pipe ceremony are considered binding and unbreakable.

Medicine men and women frequently undergo vision quests to obtain prophetic visions and to cleanse their spirits. Often people go through the sweat lodge purification ceremony before a vision quest or they take place at the same time.

Communal Celebrations

While some rituals and ceremonies are meant for a single person or small group, others include many members of a community. Celebrations such as the potlatch on the West Coast, the sun dance on the Prairies, and the powwow, traditionally involved entire communities and went on for days.

CultureLink

Cree artist Allen Sapp has captured visions of Cree life in Saskatchewan around the middle of the 20th century. The sun dance, once banned under the Indian Act, was still practised and revived by many First Nations in the mid-20th century. Many different bands would come together in the sun dance lodge. During the sun dance, prayers are said for all peoples and vows are made to the Great Spirit. Some participants would dance and fast for days to achieve visions. In part, the ceremony was a celebration of renewal and reconnection with all creation.

Figure 4-3 *Sun Dance on the Reserve* by Allen Sapp.

RECONNECT

1. Define the following terms: vision quest, sweat lodge, and sun dance, and explain the spiritual significance of each.

2. In a paragraph, explain why many Aboriginal people want to revive their traditional cultural rituals.

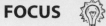
FOCUS

This section will help you understand
   a. the diversity and characteristics of Aboriginal languages
   b. factors contributing to the decline of Aboriginal languages
   c. actions which may help Aboriginal languages survive.

Language and Culture

Aboriginal cultures and languages are closely connected. There are over 50 Aboriginal languages in Canada. Each reflects the unique way Aboriginal peoples view and relate to the world. Words in a language, the ideas and feelings they represent, and the way they are spoken allow people to fully express their traditional beliefs and ways of interacting with one another. Unfortunately, many Aboriginal languages are in danger of disappearing. Recent studies, including the 1996 Royal Commission on Aboriginal Peoples, suggest that only three—Cree, Ojibway and Inuktitut—may survive as languages used in daily life.

Aboriginal peoples view the world and all it contains as an interrelated whole. They also see the world as being in a state of constant change. Many Aboriginal languages reflect this view by focusing on verbs (words which describe actions or states of being) rather than on nouns (words which identify things). For example, in the Mi'kmaq language, "trees"

> are called by the sounds they make as the wind passes through their branches, in the autumn, during the special period just before dusk. In short, they are known and talked about in terms of how they interact with certain aspects of their surroundings—and in terms of how the individual observer perceives them.

Traditionally, Aboriginal people do not describe people or things as "good" or "bad." In other words, they resist using moral labels. Their languages also do not contain words equivalent to "offender" or "criminal." These labels imply that the person has a static or unchanging nature. This would deny the Aboriginal view that the world changes constantly.

The Vital Importance of Language

…It is the native people who have the most cause to lament the passing of their languages. They lose not only the ability to express the simplest of daily sentiments and needs but they can no longer understand the ideas, concepts, insights, attitudes, rituals, ceremonies, institutions brought into being by their ancestors; and, having lost the power to understand, cannot sustain, enrich, or pass on their heritage. No longer will they think Indian or feel Indian. They will have lost their identity which no amount of reading can restore.

—Basil Johnston, "One Generation from Extinction" in *An Anthology of Native Canadian Literature in English,* eds. Daniel David Moses and Terry Goldie (Toronto: Oxford University Press Canada, 1998), pp. 99-100.

Figure 5-1   This painting by contemporary Cree artist George Littlechild tells of the importance of language to the First Nations. The caption to the painting reads: "Many First Nations languages were almost lost or annihilated. The elders tell us to learn our language and to speak it. Cree is the largest First Nation in Canada. It is important that the First Nation languages survive…."

Decline of Aboriginal Languages

Aboriginal languages have declined in use for a number of reasons. Residential schools run by missionaries were boarding schools for Aboriginal children. They were in operation from the 1840s through to the 1960s. Aboriginal children in the schools were separated from their parents and forbidden to speak their traditional languages. The languages were therefore not passed on from one generation to another. Many Aboriginal people also lost their traditional languages when they moved to urban centres to go to schools or find work. In some cases Aboriginal parents wanted to help their children fit in with Canadian society so they thought it best children were not taught their language.

Helping Aboriginal Languages Survive

Efforts are being made to keep Aboriginal languages alive. The 1996 Royal Commission on Aboriginal Peoples suggested that Aboriginal and Canadian governments take the following actions:

▶ encourage language use within families, workplaces, and communities,

▶ include Aboriginal instruction in schools and other educational programs,

▶ offer government services in Aboriginal languages,

▶ give Aboriginal languages the status of official languages in Aboriginal territories,

▶ create a foundation to work on maintaining Aboriginal languages, and

▶ include radio and television programming in Aboriginal languages in areas where significant numbers of Aboriginal people live.

Many Aboriginal communities already offer Aboriginal language classes in their schools, as do some public schools in many provinces. Aboriginal radio and television programming is also available in Aboriginal languages such as Inuktitut and Oji-Cree. Some newspapers and magazines are published in Aboriginal languages. Aboriginal centres across the country are also actively working to preserve their languages by supporting programs in schools, the publication of dictionaries and other educational materials, and community radio programs.

Figure 5-2 Aboriginal language newspapers and other publications like this one, published in English and Inuktitut, are helping to keep Aboriginal languages alive.

CultureLink

The Métis on the Prairies evolved a language called Michif. Primarily a mixture of French and Cree, it also includes elements of Chippewa, English, Gaelic, and Assiniboine. Generally, Michif combines French nouns with Cree word order and verb structures. In 1991, only 1% of the those people who identified themselves as Métis could speak Michif.

RECONNECT

1. Why are Aboriginal languages so important to Aboriginal peoples?

2. Why have many Aboriginal languages declined in use?

3. Using the list of recommendations from the Royal Commission, identify the three you believe to be the most important and explain why you consider these recommendations to be important. Use a separate sentence for each.

The Traditional Role of Elders

Elders have always played an important role in Aboriginal societies. They helped educate children. They offered practical suggestions about daily life, including the best places for hunting and fishing and ways to make household items. As keepers of traditional knowledge and history, elders also connected the community to its past by telling stories and legends. Perhaps most importantly, they acted as spiritual guides and advisors. They offered their wisdom to those who needed it and they played an important role in ceremonial practices and in community decision-making.

When the federal government and Christian churches tried to assimilate Aboriginal peoples, elders lost much of their spiritual importance in Aboriginal communities. Today, as Aboriginal peoples strive to rebuild their traditions, the role of elders has become vital once more. Once again, they participate in decision making in most Aboriginal organizations and communities.

How Does a Person Become an Elder?

To become an elder, a man or woman must have lived through many experiences to gain knowledge and wisdom. In addition to having had many experiences, an elder must also be recognized by his or her community as a wise person. Elders do not seek status. People seek them out when they need help or advice.

Most Aboriginal peoples use specific words when referring to elders. The Ojibwa call their elders the *Kichenishnabe*, which means "Great People," the Métis on the Prairies call them "Senators," and the Inuit have words which distinguish between elderly people and elders.

EyeWitness

Traditional Wisdom

In the time before the Inuvialuit had books, our elders both men and women were the keepers of Inuvialuit knowledge. Without them, each generation would have had to have learned everything there was to know by discovering it themselves. The elders also had the wisdom of age and experience. Anybody wanting to learn had only to sit and listen to an elder speak. The hunters especially relied heavily upon the stories and advice given by their elders so they could become better hunters and leaders… In the old age, … [the elders] had more time to observe the people of their camp as they went about their daily routines. Based upon their observations, they would give advice to the young and old… "Baby, you must not kick that seal even though it is dead. It is our food and you must respect it." "Young man, don't get angry so easily. Try to forget what happened." Sometimes they would tell stories. The stories would always help the young people to learn about ways of doing things and ways of behaving. Their words were full of information and wisdom and our people respected the elders.

—Northwest Territories Department of Education, *Inuvialuit Pitqusiit*.

Figure 6-1 Today, elders in Aboriginal communities are helping young people to connect with their heritages and learn traditional ways.

What do Elders do Today?

Elders connect people to the events, customs and ceremonies of the past. Therefore they must have a strong knowledge of traditional Aboriginal ways. This role has become very important in many Aboriginal communities.

Elders also act as counsellors but they do not impose their knowledge and wisdom. Typically, people must ask the elder for his or her insights. Elders listen patiently and non-judgmentally. They combine spiritual views, which may be focused around traditional or Christian beliefs, with their experience of life to provide suggestions or make observations.

Elders perform these roles both on reserves and in urban settings. Most First Nations communities try to involve elders in decision making. The Assembly of First Nations, for example, has a Council of Elders which offers guidance to the National Chief and the First Nations-in-Assembly.

Recently, elders have also become important

Figure 6-2   Elders play an important role in the performance of ceremonies and in decision-making in Aboriginal communities.

mediators in criminal proceedings involving Aboriginal people. The elders offer guidance about sentencing and suggestions about how to reintegrate offenders back into their communities. Elders also go into prisons to counsel Aboriginal offenders and help them reconnect to their heritage by performing rituals such as the sweat lodge.

CaseStudy

THE ROLE OF ELDERS IN URBAN CENTRES

Aboriginal people face many challenges when they move from their reserves or traditional homelands to Canadian towns and cities. In particular, they face the challenge of keeping their Aboriginal language, culture, and traditions. To help, many Aboriginal social organizations in cities employ elders. The Native Canadian Centre of Toronto asks elders to advise and guide both the organization and the people who come to the Centre. Elders who work in urban centres face particular challenges because the Aboriginal people they meet often come from many different First Nations and have many different cultural backgrounds.

What do elders do at the Centre?
► Counsel individuals and groups.
► Teach about Aboriginal ways.
► Perform ceremonies.
► Provide knowledge of Aboriginal healing.
► Advise the organization.
► Help with conflict resolution.
► Act as role models.
► Provide a spiritual presence.

What qualities does the Centre want an elder to have?
► Live an Aboriginal lifestyle.
► Commit to helping the Aboriginal community (possibly without pay).
► Have experience of life.
► Have a thorough knowledge of traditions and ceremonies.
► Commit to improving the quality of life in the Aboriginal community.
► Be a good communicator, preferably with Aboriginal language skills.
► Have a proven ability to work with people, especially young people.
► Understand the challenges Aboriginal people face in an urban setting.
► Be patient and non-judgmental.

—*Based on the requirements of the Native Canadian Centre in Toronto.*

RECONNECT

1. a. Identify four qualities an elder must possess.
   b. Suggest reasons why elders must possess each of these qualities.

2. In a paragraph, describe the role of an elder in an urban setting. Use specific examples.

Traditional Family Patterns

Traditionally, Aboriginal peoples lived in small communities where the family played an extremely important role. Often the family was an extended group which included parents and children as well as grandparents, aunts, and uncles. Among many Aboriginal peoples such as the Cree and Inuit, extended families spent much of the year together hunting in a close-knit group. Family members all had roles to play in daily life and they depended on one another.

In some Aboriginal cultures, families also belonged to specific clans. For example, the Mohawks divided families into the Wolf, Turtle, and Bear clans, while the Haida had two clans—the Raven and the Eagle. The clan a family belonged to had great significance. A clan often had specific traditional hunting areas. Clan membership also affected a person's relationship with the spirit world and social status within the community.

In some communities, clans defined the roles and responsibilities of individuals. In many First Nations communities, only individuals from particular clans could rise to leadership positions or become healers. The Seneca of the Haudenosaunee (Iroquois) Confederacy had nine clans but only six could elect chiefs to the council. People from different communities often belonged to the same clan. In this way, clans helped to unite Aboriginal peoples. Clans are still important among many First Nations today.

Raising Children

In most traditional Aboriginal cultures, children were considered gifts from the spirit world and were celebrated. In early childhood, Aboriginal children learned by observing older people in a variety of activities including hunting, carving, weaving, or performing ceremonies. The children gained a rich store of knowledge about history, geography, botany,

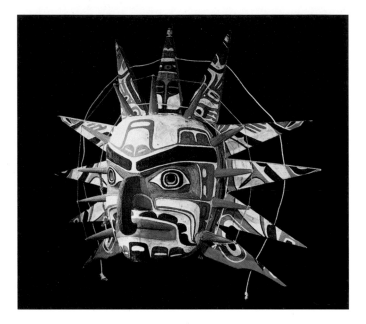

Figure 7-1 This mask represents the sun, which was the main crest of the Sisinlae family lineage of the Nimpkish clan at Alert Bay. The right to this crest would be explained in a origin myth involving an ancestor and the sun.

astronomy, language, and spiritual teachings. They developed a sense of morality through observation and through listening to stories and legends. Parents and elders modelled appropriate behaviour and encouraged children to be responsible to the group. Elders would watch children to see who showed special interests or skills. Then they would encourage those children and provide opportunities for them to develop their skills.

Government Policies and Changing Family Patterns

Government policies and other social pressures have had a profound impact on Aboriginal families.

▶ From the 1840s to the 1960s, residential schools removed children from their families; as a result, many children could no longer fit into traditional lifestyles on reserves, nor could they adjust to non-Aboriginal society.

Figure 7-2 *Father Image I*, 1991 by Jim Logan. In this painting two boys interrupt their game to have their picture taken with a priest at a residential school. Children were often sent to residential schools at ages as young as five or six. They often did not return home for many years, losing contact with their parents. The priest often became a father figure to these children.

Figure 7-3 *Father Image II*, 1991, by Jim Logan. This painting is of Jim Logan and his father, a Métis who fought for Canada in WW II. Father and son are enjoying a hockey game together. What point do you think the artist is making in these two paintings?

▶ Many Aboriginal people have experienced poverty, inadequate and substandard housing, and poor health care on reserves. For most of the 20th century, child mortality rates for Aboriginal people ranged two or three times that of the total Canadian population.

▶ Social welfare agencies tried to deal with such problems in the 1960s by removing Aboriginal children from their birth families and putting them into foster care. For example, in British Columbia in 1955, less than 1% of the children dealt with by social welfare agencies were Aboriginal, but by 1964, 34% were Aboriginal. With time, the situation only grew worse. In 1980, Aboriginal children accounted for 36.7 % of all children in care, but were only 3.5% of all children in the province. The situation in other provinces was much the same. Most social welfare agencies also put the children up for adoption into non-Aboriginal households against the wishes of their parents; this practice continued until the 1980s.

Poverty, high rates of unemployment, and social breakdown have led to problems such as substance abuse, family violence, and sexual abuse. Aboriginal peoples have tried to combat these problems by establishing healing centres and by creating Aboriginal child welfare agencies to keep Aboriginal children within extended families. Although the problems do not affect all Aboriginal people, they do exist and in many cases are quite severe.

Primary Source

Traditional values such as respect for all people and living things, a strong sense of family and community, caring, sharing and encouraging each other: these are our most important values. We must cherish our values; which are the basis of our strength as individuals and as First Nations and keep them close to our hearts.

—*Pauline Pelly, Keeseekoose First Nation Elder and past Counsellor with the Saskatchewan Indian Technologies Institute, 1996*, Saskatchewan Indian Cultural Centre, Saskatechwan Elders Site www.sicc.sk.ca

RECONNECT

1. Why was family life so important in traditional Aboriginal culture?

2. Identify three ways that government policies affected Aboriginal families.

3. What steps are Aboriginal people taking to combat problems caused by past government policies?

FOCUS 💡

This section will help you understand
   a. the variety of government forms in traditional Aboriginal communities and nations
   b. how traditional Aboriginal governments have evolved.

Traditional Governments

Just as the cultures and languages of Aboriginal peoples vary across Canada, so do their traditional systems of government. Despite the differences, Aboriginal communities and nations shared some common principles of government. Most Aboriginal societies valued individual responsibility and independence, but they also believed in the importance of sharing. For example, while everyone had an individual responsibility, food and resources were shared, especially in times of need. Cooperation was key and consensus (group agreement) was a central part of decision-making.

In most First Nations, leaders earned their authority and had to be responsive to the needs and wishes of their people. Among the Siksika (Blackfoot), leaders gained recognition and authority on the basis of their courage, generosity, honesty, and wisdom. They governed only as long as they had the confidence of their people. Leadership was informal, and there were no elections.

Governments Today

In 1869, the federal government introduced elected band councils in order to discourage traditional Aboriginal government. The band council system has been continued under the Indian Act. Today, the councils control most of the social services provided on reserves including housing and education. Although the federal government kept control over the band councils for many years, by 1996 the councils had control over 83% of the budget of the Department of Indian and Northern Affairs. Recently, more and more communities are also determining their own leadership selection process.

Today Aboriginal peoples are continuing to work for self-government. Some are considering a return to traditional government forms. Others are adopting new forms of government while incorporating some of the values and principles of their traditional societies.

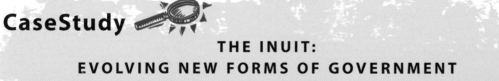

CaseStudy 🔍

THE INUIT:
EVOLVING NEW FORMS OF GOVERNMENT

Traditionally, the Inuit lived in bands made up of several families. The bands did not formally choose chiefs, but each band had a leader. The leader was known as the *angajuqqaaq*, "the one who is listened to and obeyed," or the *isumataq*, "the one who thinks."

Among the Iglulingmiut of Baffin Island, the eldest hunter in a band usually became the *isumataq* and made decisions about food sharing which affected the entire camp. Among the Netsilingmiut of Hudson Bay, a group of men, usually related, shared most decisions. In Copper Inuit communities, men and women enjoyed relatively similar degrees of influence. Only when Inuit bands came together for whale hunts or to defend themselves against others did they choose a main leader. Otherwise Inuit cultures did not have a central authority or government. Rules and laws were not written down, but elders reinforced social rules and all members of a band participated in publicly shaming rule breakers.

In 1939, the Inuit were made the responsibility of the federal government. Their traditional lifestyles were shattered. Recently, with land claims agreements in the North, some Inuit are regaining the right to govern themselves. In the territory of Nunavut, the Inuit form a majority. They have decided on the form of government in the territory. Since their traditional lifestyle has changed, the Inuit have adopted a more centralized form of government and have accepted elections for choosing leaders to represent them. Decision makers, however, will still be guided by elders. (Read more about Nunavut on page 66.)

Figure 8-1   Inuit leader Zebedee Nungak has been active in the struggle for self-government in the region of Northern Quebec (north of 53° latitude) which the Inuit call Nunavik. New forms of government are still evolving.

CaseStudy

THE HAUDENOSAUNEE (IROQUOIS CONFEDERACY): THE STRUGGLE FOR SOVEREIGNTY

The history of the Haudenosaunee tells of the Great Peacemaker, Dekanawideh. Before the arrival of the Europeans, Dekanawideh brought a message of peace to five Iroquois nations, the Mohawk, Oneida, Onondaga, Cayuga, and Seneca. The Tuscaroras joined the Confederacy in 1715 and since that time it has also been known as the Six Nations.

Dekanawideh created the constitution of the Confederacy known as the Great Law of Peace. The Great Law of Peace was a code of living, ranging from laws on governing to how to behave in society. The Great Law established a council of chiefs with representatives, called sachems, from each nation. While each nation still had control over its own internal affairs, the council discussed issues such as trade, alliances, treaties, and war that affected all members.

All decisions of the council were reached by general agreement or consensus and all nations had to agree before a decision was passed. Every chief had the right to speak, but the most senior chiefs usually spoke last so they could incorporate the ideas of others. Clan mothers from each nation nominated eligible chiefs from the clan to represent the nation. The clan mothers could remove a chief if he failed to represent the interests of his people. Each chief therefore needed to consult with his people to reflect their wishes.

Since the late 1800s, many communities of the Haudenosaunee have been divided between supporters of the traditional governments and those who have adopted the elected band council the government required by the Indian Act. Despite these disagreements, the people have continually asserted their **sovereignty** throughout their history. They claim the right to determine their own form of government without the interference of the Canadian or U.S. governments.

> **The Great Law of Peace**
> The Great Law is an oral law and narrating it can take many days. This is a short excerpt.
>
> The Word that I bring is that all peoples shall love one another and live together in peace. This message has three parts: Righteousness and Health and Power—Gàiwoh, Skénon, Gashasdénshaa. And each part has two branches.
> Righteousness means justice practised between men and between nations; it means also a desire to see justice prevail. Health means soundness of mind and body; it also means peace, for that is what comes when minds are sane and bodies are cared for.
> Power means authority of law and custom, backed by such force as is necessary to make justice prevail; it means also religion, for justice enforced is the will of the Holder of the Heavens and has his sanction.

▶ The Haudenosaunee assert that they were the first union of American states and the first participatory democracy on the continent; when political leaders were drawing up the Constitution of the United States in the 1780s, they took ideas from the Haudenosaunee Constitution and their government structure.

▶ They believe that treaties signed with early European nations are proof that these European nations recognized the Haudenosaunee as sovereign nations; evidence of these treaties are found in wampum belts and the oral histories of the Six Nations.

▶ Various Haudenosaunee councils issued their own declarations of war against Germany during World War I.

▶ The Haudenosaunee of the Six Nations Reserve issue their own passports which are recognized by 36 nations around the world.

▶ The people continue to send representatives on international missions to assert their claim to self-government.

Figure 8-2 *Turtle Island* by Mohawk artist Stanley R. Hill. Carved of moose antler and wood, this piece depicts the creation of the world and the founding of the Haudenosaunee Confederacy. It shows the Tree of Peace, the central symbol of the Confederacy. An eagle hovers above the tree. The eagle was considered a very wise bird that could see far into the distance and represents strength, power and clearness of sight.

RECONNECT

1. Describe how leaders were chosen in each of the three Aboriginal groups discussed in this section: the Siksika, the Inuit, and the Haudenosaunee.

2. What impact has the Canadian federal government had on Aboriginal forms of government?

FOCUS

This section will help you understand
a. the variety and purpose of traditional dance and music forms
b. recent developments in Aboriginal music and dance.

Dance: From Traditional to Modern

In many traditional Aboriginal cultures, dancing was important in grand ceremonials and private curing rites. Many dances were passed along from generation to generation, while others were newly created for each performance. Some came from vision experiences. Many Aboriginal peoples had dancing societies that kept the knowledge of the dances and possessed the right to present specific dance cycles as parts of spiritual events or at social gatherings. Today, many traditional dances are still performed, while some have evolved over time into new forms.

Dances have many different purposes: healing and curing, celebrating animal and other natural spirits, renewal and thanksgiving, birth and marriage, greeting, joy and mourning, even clowning. Often dancing is a way to get in touch with the spirit world. The sun dance, an important celebration among the First Nations of the Prairies, and dances associated with the potlatch on the West Coast were banned by the Canadian government in the late 1800s because the government considered these dances "backward." Still, many dances survived and are performed at modern powwows when First Nations gather to renew social and spiritual ties and celebrate traditions. Some powwow dances are social, others competitive. Other dances are sacred and are not performed in public.

Figure 9-1 Some dances included elaborate costumes and masks.

CultureLink

SACRED MASKED DANCES

Some dances included elaborate masks and costumes. Sacred rituals preserved by the nations of the Haudenosaunee (Iroquois) involve the mask societies known as the False Faces (called *Gagohsa* or mask among the Seneca, *Gagu:wara* or face among the Mohawk, *Hadu?i* or hunchback among the Onondaga). The masks of the Iroquois are considered so sacred that it is dishonourable to photograph them. Each mask is different, based on the carver's imagination. Sometimes, carvers create the faces from their dreams or visions. The masks represent powerful healing spirits which live in the forest. During the Traveling Rite in spring and autumn, the masked dancers heal by blowing hot ashes on the sick. At the beginning of the midwinter festival, they sing and dance and seek offerings of tobacco and food to honour the protective spirits.

There are many stories about the origins of the masks. One legend tells of how the Creator Hawenniyo once met and challenged the Great False Face, leader of all the False Faces in the forest, to a contest. Whoever could call the distant mountain to him would be the winner. Hawenniyo calls the mountain and it comes directly to him. The Great False Face calls the mountain and it moves only a short distance, but in turning around to see he smashes his nose against the rock. Many of the masks portray the bent nose and distorted face.

Still, Hawenniyo recognizes the False Face's great power. The False Face agrees that if people make masks of him, offer tobacco, and honour him in their rituals, he will give them the power to cure diseases. Mask makers still honour the spirit. The masks are carved out roughly at first from the trunk of a living tree, and then the block is cut from the tree and the details of the mask are completed.

Traditional Music

Music holds a central place in Aboriginal cultures. Songs connect people to each other and to the spirit world. Some songs are ritualistic, handed down within families or special societies, while others are newly composed fresh after a vision or crucial life experience.

Aboriginal music varies across Canada. Music among the Inuit, for example, includes unaccompanied throat singing or *katajjaq*—a form of musical game in which pairs of women face each other at a close distance and sing rapid repetitive guttural sounds. Aboriginal music from the Plains includes groups of male singers performing high pitched songs while accompanying themselves with loud rhythmic drumming. Despite the differences in musical styles, some common elements exist: song lyrics tend to use nature imagery, repetition, and vocables—syllables of sound. Accompaniments include drums made of stretched skins or wooden planks, rattles, and flutes.

New Aboriginal Music

Aboriginal performers have also been well represented in more mainstream music in Canada. Folk singer Buffy Sainte-Marie has had a long, successful career while championing Aboriginal music. Songwriter and composer Robbie Robertson has established an international career working with performers such as Ronnie Hawkins and Bob Dylan, writing the scores for movies such as *Raging Bull*, and as a solo performer. Other successful Aboriginal performers include Inuit singer and songwriter Susan Aglukark and the Innu band Kashtin.

Less well known is composer Barbara Croall, who received the prestigious Glenn Gould prize for composition in 1989. Her works incorporate Aboriginal languages and themes but draw on the Western tradition of classical music. Also highly respected in the music field is John Kim Bell, the first Aboriginal conductor.

BIOGRAPHY

Figure 9-2 Susan Aglukark.

Subject: Susan Aglukark

Dates: Born in Churchill, Manitoba in 1967

Most Notable Accomplishment: Successful singer and songwriter whose music interweaves both English and Inuktitut and addresses Inuit concerns. Winner of the first Aboriginal Achievement Award in the Arts & Entertainment field in 1994 and of two Juno Awards in 1995.

Thumbnail Sketch: For the first 12 years of her life, Susan Aglukark moved around the Northwest Territories with her father (a minister), mother, and seven brothers and sisters. They later settled in Arviat, N.W.T., on the shore of Hudson Bay where Susan completed high school. Moving to Ottawa, she worked for the Department of Indian and Northern Affairs as a linguist and then as an executive assistant with the Inuit Tapirisat, the political and cultural organization that represents the Inuit. Following her first live performance in her home town, she launched her musical career. In 1992, she released her first independent recording *Arctic Rose*, which became a major success. In 1993, she signed a worldwide recording contract. Her music combines both traditional Inuit chants and themes with contemporary pop melodies. While reviving and celebrating traditional rituals and values, she also sings about the social realities of life in today's North, including the clash of cultures and youth suicide. Susan Aglukark has worked as National Spokesperson for the Aboriginal Division of the National Alcohol and Drug Prevention Program.

Significant Quote: "A line in the song *'siem o siyeya'* means all peoples, all cultures and races, all people rich and poor. The song talks about watching the walls come tumbling down, and by that I mean the walls of racism and prejudice, of hate and anger."

RECONNECT

1. Explain the importance of traditional dances in Aboriginal cultures.

2. How do contemporary musicians incorporate Aboriginal traditions into their music?

FOCUS 💡

This section will help you understand
a. the variety and purpose of traditional Aboriginal arts
b. how exposure to non-Aboriginal culture has affected Aboriginal art
c. the challenges of being an Aboriginal artist and the issues surrounding Aboriginal art today.

Art and Life

Aboriginal peoples have decorated their personal possessions and created sacred and ceremonial objects for thousands of years. They embroidered their clothing, carved designs in bowls and utensils, and created elaborate basketry. They also expressed their spiritual beliefs in sacred and ceremonial objects such as finely crafted masks and pipes. Their artistic creations were a direct expression of their cultures and everyday lives.

Before the 20th century, the majority of Aboriginal artworks could be carried or worn since most people lived in small family groups that moved around their territories with the seasons. On the West Coast, where First Nations were more settled because of an abundance of food year round, people created massive artworks such as canoes, totem poles, and decorated houses. Each used materials from its environment. On the West Coast, for example, First Nations used cedar for carving as well as for clothing and utensils. Each First Nation also used specific designs, symbols, and techniques which expressed its beliefs, values, and history.

Figure 10-1a Mi'kmaq quillwork boxes. Mi'kmaq women crafted boxes, dishes, and baskets out of porcupine quills.

Figure 10-1b This Dene dress was made in the late 19th century out of moosehide, velveteen, beads, and tin tinklers.

Figure 10-1c A copy of a traditional Sto:lo Nation mask. It is carved from red cedar and depicts a type of duck called a merganser.

Traditions Evolve

Contact with non-Aboriginal people has affected Aboriginal art forms in a number of ways:

▶ At the time of contact, European trade goods such as glass beads and metal were incorporated into artworks.

▶ When government regulations banned traditional ceremonies such as the potlatch, the arts associated with these ceremonies were sometimes lost, forgotten, or put in museums.

▶ With widespread death from disease and attempts to change Aboriginal peoples' way of life, skills and traditions were no longer passed on from one generation to another. In some cases, the traditional meaning and spiritual value of some designs almost disappeared and had to be relearned from artworks collected in museums.

▶ Some artists changed traditional designs to make them more popular with tourists or collectors.

▶ Artists adopted new techniques, materials, and styles as they were exposed to new ideas.

Contemporary Issues

Many artists of Aboriginal ancestry still create traditional art forms. Others are exploring new areas or searching for a way to balance their heritage with their desire for more individual artistic expression. Some even question whether Aboriginal artists should be expected to use traditional designs or address issues facing Aboriginal peoples.

Primary Source

Art was one with the culture. Art was our only written language. It documented our progress as a people, it documented the histories of the families. Throughout our history, it has been the art that has kept our spirit alive.

There are more people who want to get involved in Native art now. It has been a catalyst in re-connecting people with their cultural identity. And it's made people more aware of Native people and issues.

—Haida artist Robert Davidson quoted in *Eagle of the Dawn*, ed. M. Ian Thom (Vancouver: Vancouver Art Gallery, 1993), p. 8.

Recently some Aboriginal people have also become concerned about non-Aboriginal people using traditional Aboriginal stories and designs for their own purposes. They consider this use of Aboriginal art forms a "theft" of Aboriginal culture and call it **cultural appropriation**. They also worry about non-Aboriginal people telling Aboriginal history or using Aboriginal characters in fictional works such as novels and movies.

Many Aboriginal people also argue that museums and collectors should return Aboriginal artifacts to their original communities. They say that museums often acquired the art by confiscation (without permission) and worry that museums will not display Aboriginal cultural objects in an appropriate way.

Figure 10-2 *Elitekey* by contemporary Mi'kmaq artist Teresa Marshall. The three figures are sculpted from cement. The artist has combined traditional elements—a Mi'kmaq canoe and a figure in traditional dress—with a contemporary Canadian flag, suggesting a questioning of identity.

Figure 10-3 Contemporary Cree artist Jane Ash Poitras has painted several pieces exploring the importance of spiritual guidance. This print is titled *Pink Shaman*.

CaseStudy

WEST COAST ART

People around the world recognize the distinctive Aboriginal art from the West Coast. Traditional West Coast First Nations had an elaborate social structure with classes that ranged from chiefs through nobles, commoners, and slaves. They also had a rich ceremonial life that continues today. The artwork produced in these societies reflected these social classes and spiritual beliefs. Totem poles, for example, contain family crests and describe family histories and honours, while clothing designs on Chilkat capes vary according to social class. Masks, woven baskets and clothing, jewellery, rattles, feast dishes, talking sticks and many other objects of the West Coast First Nations reflect the variety and imaginative forms of their art.

West Coast societies also had groups of professional artists who were commissioned to create works for potlatches and winter ceremonies by wealthy **patrons**. The artists were trained from youth by master artists, in most cases their uncles or fathers.

The arrival of Europeans on the West Coast brought many changes. With the introduction of iron tools, totem poles became larger and more elaborate. New materials were also introduced. Hudson's Bay blankets and buttons led Aboriginal women to create a new art form: the button decorated cape. Paints were replaced with European products. These changes, along with increased wealth from trade, led to a creative boom in the arts during the 19th century.

In the 20th century, depopulation from disease, the outlawing of practices such as the potlatch, residential schooling, and new values introduced by Christian churches sent West Coast art into decline. Although artists such as Willie Seaweed and Charles Edenshaw kept the traditions alive in the early 20th century, West Coast art remained in decline until the 1960s.

Stirrings of revival began in the 1940s and 1950s with the work of Mungo Martin and Henry Hunt. They were commissioned by the provincial government of British Columbia to repair old artworks, to create new ones, and to teach a new generation of artists. This new generation, which includes Tony and Richard Hunt, Doug Cranmer, Bill Reid and Robert Davidson, came to prominence in the 1960s. Many of these artists had to teach themselves the symbolism of the past because so many of the traditional works and skills had been forgotten or lost. They often studied pieces in museums to relearn the old ways. They also adapted traditional symbols and introduced new materials such as gold, silver, and bronze in their work.

Figure 10-4 West Coast artists combined European buttons and cloth to make button blankets that showed traditional symbols in new styles.

Figure 10-5   Raising of Robert Davidson's totem pole in 1969.

In 1969, Haida artist Robert Davidson raised the first new totem pole in the Queen Charlotte Islands since the banning of the potlatch in 1884. By the 1980s, an estimated 200 artists were working in all the former styles and many had gained international reputations. Today, these artists are once again training apprentices. They have been leaders in the cultural revival of First Nations on the West Coast.

"Carving my first totem pole helped me to connect with culture. For many years before that art was only made for sale in the curio market. There was no ceremony, no masks. That totem pole was so foreign that none of the elders, none of the oldest people, had witnessed a pole raising. It woke up a lot of people, including myself. I didn't realize the impact it would have."

—*Robert Davidson quoted in Barbara Hager,* Honour Song: A Tribute *(Vancouver: Raincoast Books, 1996), p. 5.*

Inuit Art

Inuit art has gone through a unique evolution. Traditionally, Inuit decorated their utensils and their clothing. Parka decorations, for example, varied across the Arctic and could be used to identify particular Inuit groups. Inuit also produced small carvings using bone, wood, and ivory. Soapstone was used primarily for pots and lamps.

In 1948 James Houston, an artist, lecturer and associate of the Canadian Handicrafts Guild, travelled to northern Quebec at the request of the federal government to collect Inuit carvings. In the next few years, he encouraged sculptors to produce soapstone carvings for sale. Then in 1957, Houston introduced printmaking to the Inuit in Cape Dorset on Baffin Island. Today, both these art forms have become highly prized by collectors and are a main source of income for many Inuit. As with soapstone carvings, subjects for prints include animals, daily Inuit life, and mythical beings.

Figure 10-6 Kenojuak Ashevak is one of the most recognized Inuit sculptors and print makers. She has received an Aboriginal Achievement Award for her work. This print is titled *Arrival of the Spirit.*

EyeWitness

Museums return sacred objects

Recently, some museums such as the Royal Ontario Museum and the Glenbow Museum in Alberta have returned objects to Aboriginal communities or signed agreements allowing bands to use the objects. Others, such as the Vancouver Museum have consulted Aboriginal people and asked them to be **curators** when they display Aboriginal art. First Nations are continuing to work towards recovering or replacing these lost aspects of their cultures and pasts.

We do not have a word for repatriation in the Kwak'wala language. The closest we come to it is the word u'mista, which… means the return of something important. We are working towards u'mista of much that was almost lost to us. The return of the potlatch collection is one u'mista. The renewed interest among younger people in learning about their cultural history is a kind of u'mista. The creation of new ceremonial gear to replace that held by museums is yet another u'mista. We are taking back, from many sources, information about our culture and our history, to help us rebuild our world which was almost shattered during the bad times.

—Gloria Cranmer Webster, "From Colonization to Repatriation" in *Indigena: Contemporary Native Perspectives,* eds. Gerald McMaster and Lee-Ann Marin (Ottawa: Douglas and McIntyre and Canadian Museum of Civilization, 1992), p. 37.

RECONNECT

1. Identify three ways that exposure to non-Aboriginal culture affected Aboriginal art and provide a specific example of each.

2. What contemporary issues concern some Aboriginal artists?

3. What positive actions led to a revival in Aboriginal art? Be specific.

FOCUS

This section will help you understand
  a. the importance of traditional storytelling in Aboriginal cultures
  b. the themes and varieties of contemporary Aboriginal literature.

The Tradition

Traditional stories, legends, songs, history, and all other forms of knowledge were passed on from one generation to another by constant retelling. A wide range of songs, chants, dramas, poems, and prayers were also kept as parts of ceremonies practised for centuries. Spiritual leaders, elders, members of dance and medicine societies and others kept the knowledge of these spoken forms in their memories.

At the end of the 19th century and the beginning of the 20th century, ethnographers began visiting Aboriginal communities across Canada and recording traditional stories, songs, and legends. Recently, Aboriginal people have also been actively recording their oral heritage and have added to it, creating new forms as they write of their experiences in the contemporary world.

Contemporary Aboriginal writer Thomas King suggests that while traditional stories and legends remained oral, they had very particular audiences, namely those who spoke a given language. He believes their translation into European languages helped introduce the stories to other Aboriginal groups and to non-Aboriginal people. It may also have helped preserve the stories by reinforcing their importance across Aboriginal cultures.

CONNECTIONS

TWO POEMS ACROSS THE CENTURIES

One of the first well-known Aboriginal writers in the 20th century was Emily Pauline Johnson, Tekahionwake, a Mohawk. Rita Joe is a contemporary Mi'kmaq poet who has written several books. The two poems below span decades. What common themes can you see?

Corn Husker
Hard by the Indian lodges, where the bush
  Breaks in a clearing, through ill-fashioned fields.
She comes to labour, when the first still hush
  Of autumn follows large and recent yields.

Age in her fingers, hunger on her face,
  Her shoulders stooped with weight of work and years,
But rich in tawny colouring of her race,
  She comes a-field to strip the purple ears.

And all her thoughts are with the days gone by,
  Ere might's injustice banished from their lands
Her people, that to-day unheeded lie,
  Like the dead husks that rustle through her hands.

—Pauline Johnson
(Tekahionwake)

Figure 11-1
Mohawk poet
Pauline Johnson.

untitled poem
They say that I must live
a white man's way.
This day and age
Still being bent to what they say,
My heart remains
Tuned to native time.

I must dress conservative in style
And have factory shoes upon my feet.
Leave the ways they say
Are wild.
Forfeit a heritage
That is conquered.

I must accept what this century
Has destroyed and left behind—
The innocence of my ancestry.

I must forget father sky
And mother earth,
And hurt this land we love
With towering concrete.

—Rita Joe

Figure 11-2
Mi'kmaq poet
Rita Joe.

Modern Aboriginal Writing

Aboriginal writing today is a vibrant and growing new body of literature. A surge of modern writing, focusing attention on Aboriginal concerns, began in the 1960s and 1970s. Key publications included *The Unjust Society* (1971) by Harold Cardinal which reacted strongly against government proposals to change the special rights of Aboriginal peoples outlined in the **White Paper** Policy of 1969. (See pages 58–59.) *Halfbreed* (1973) by Maria Campbell, was a stirring memoir of her personal struggles and the struggles of the Métis people.

Since then Aboriginal writers have produced poetry, novels, essays and plays and have become an important and distinctive part of the Canadian literary scene. Some of the most well known include Emma LaRoque, Lee Maracle, Jeanette Armstrong, Ruby Slipperjack, Thomas King, Drew Hayden Taylor, and playwright Tomson Highway. While the works of these contemporary writers vary, each presents Aboriginal life and life in Canada from an Aboriginal perspective.

Figure 11-3
Thomas King.

Some works contain humour and incorporate traditional figures from Aboriginal legends such as the trickster. Others show the tragic side of some Aboriginal lives including abuse, suicide and discrimination. Whether or not contemporary Aboriginal literary works incorporate traditional figures or Aboriginal people, they tend to celebrate traditional Aboriginal concerns such as nature, community and family life, and the interrelatedness of life.

CultureLink
REINTERPRETING TRADITIONS

Aboriginal legends typically explain the creation of the world and the relationships among people, the land, and the spirit world. One of the key figures in legends is the trickster-transformer. Human or animal, he is known to various First Nations under different names: Raven among Pacific Coast First Nations, Coyote or "old man" among the Plains peoples, Nanabozho to the Ojibwa, and Glooscap to the Mi'kmaq. The trickster is sometimes creator and helper, sometimes joker or crafty trickster who can transform himself into animal and human shapes, but who sometimes falls victim to his own and others' tricks. To Aboriginal peoples, the delicate balance of the universe is constantly changing and can be upset. Humans need to constantly work to maintain the harmony and keep the spirits positive. In the following short story, writer Thomas King draws on the traditional character of the trickster to present a contemporary Aboriginal interpretation of history.

Read the story two or three times. Think about these questions as you read.
- What is the relationship between Coyote and Old Coyote?
- How does Old Coyote play the role of trickster, transformer, and Creator? How does she fall victim to her own tricks?
- What does Christopher Columbus and his taking of the Indians symbolize? How are past and present interwoven in this story?
- How is humour used in this story?
- How do the style and themes of this story compare with those in the two poems presented earlier?

A Coyote Columbus Story

You know, Coyote came by my place the other day. She was going to a party. She had her party hat and she had her party whistle and she had her party rattle.

> I'm going to a party, she says.

> Yes, I says, I can see that.

> It is a party for Christopher Columbus, says Coyote.

That is the one who found America. That is the one who found Indians.

Boy, that Coyote is one silly Coyote. You got to watch out for her. Some of Coyote's stories have got Coyote tails and some of Coyote's stories are covered with scraggy Coyote fur but all of Coyote's stories are bent.

Christopher Columbus didn't find America, I says. Christopher Columbus didn't find Indians, either. You got a tail on that story.

Oh no, says Coyote. I read it in a book.

Must have been a Coyote book, I says.

No, no, no, no, says Coyote. It was a history book. Big red one. All about how Christopher Columbus sailed the ocean blue looking for America and the Indians.

Sit down, I says. Have some tea. We're going to have to do this story right. We're going to have to do this story now.

It was all Old Coyote's fault, I tell Coyote, and here is how the story goes. Here is what really happened.

So.

Old Coyote loved to play ball, you know. She played ball all day and all night. She would throw the ball and she would hit the ball and she would run and catch the ball. But playing ball by herself was boring, so she sang a song and she danced a dance and she thought about playing ball and pretty soon along came some Indians. Old Coyote and the Indians became very good friends. You are sure a good friend, says those Indians. Yes, that's true, says Old Coyote.

But, you know, whenever Old Coyote and the Indians played ball, Old Coyote always won. She always won because she made up the rules. That sneaky one made up the rules and she always won because she could do that.

That's not fair, says the Indians. Friends don't do that.

That's the rules, says Old Coyote. Let's play some more. Maybe you will win the next time. But they don't.

You keep changing the rules, says those Indians.

No, no, no, no, says Old Coyote. You are mistaken. And then she changes the rules again.

So, after a while, those Indians find better things to do.

Some of them go fishing.

Some of them go shopping.

Some of them go to a movie.

Some of them go on a vacation.

Those Indians got better things to do than play ball with Old Coyote and those changing rules.

So, Old Coyote doesn't have anyone to play with.

So, she has to play by herself.

So, she gets bored.

When Old Coyote gets bored, anything can happen. Stick around. Big trouble is coming, I can tell you that.

Well. That silly one sings a song and she dances a dance and she thinks about playing ball. But she's thinking about changing those rules, too, and she doesn't watch what she is making up out of her head.

So pretty soon, she makes three ships.

Hmmmm, says Old Coyote, where did those ships come from?

And pretty soon, she makes some people on those ships.

Hmmmm, says Old Coyote, where did those people come from?

And pretty soon, she makes some people on the beach with flags and funny-looking clothes and stuff.

Hooray, says Old Coyote. You are just in time for the ball game.

Hello, says one of the men in silly clothes and red hair all over his head. I am Christopher Columbus. I am sailing the ocean blue looking for China. Have you seen it?

Forget China, says Old Coyote. Let's play ball.

It must be around here somewhere, says Christopher Columbus. I have a map.

Forget the map, says Old Coyote. I'll bat first and I'll tell you the rules as we go along.

But that Christopher Columbus and his friends don't want to play ball. We got work to do, he says. We got to find China. We got to find things we can sell.

Yes, says those Columbus people, where is the gold?

Yes, they says, where is that silk cloth?

Yes, they says, where are those portable color televisions?

Yes, they says, where are those home computers?

Boy, says Old Coyote, and that one scratches her head. I must have sung that song wrong. Maybe I didn't do the right dance. Maybe I thought too hard. These people I made have no manners. They act as if they have no relations.

And she is right. Christopher Columbus and his friends start jumping up and down in their funny clothes and they shout so loud that Coyote's ears almost fall off.

Boy, what a bunch of noise, say Coyote. What bad manners. You guys got to stop jumping and shouting or my ears will fall off.

We got to find China, says Christopher Columbus. We got to become rich. We got to become famous. Do you think you can help us?

But all Old Coyote can think about is playing ball. I'll let you bat first, say Old Coyote.

No time for games, says Christopher Columbus.

I'll let you make the rules, cries Old Coyote.

But those Columbus people don't listen. They are too busy running around, peeking under rocks, looking in caves, sailing all over the place. Looking for China. Looking for stuff they can sell.

I got a monkey, says one.

I got a parrot, says another.

I got a fish, says a third.

I got a coconut, says a fourth.

That stuff isn't worth poop, says Christopher Columbus. We can't sell those things in Spain. Look harder.

But all they find are monkeys and parrots and fish and coconuts. And when they tell Christopher Columbus, that one he squeezes his ears and he chews his nose and grinds his teeth. He grinds his teeth so hard, he gets a headache, and then, he gets cranky.

And then he gets an idea.

Say, says Christopher Columbus. Maybe we could sell Indians.

Yes, says his friends, that's a good idea. We could sell Indians, and they throw away their monkeys and parrots and fish and coconuts.

Wait a minute, says the Indians, that is not a good idea. That is a bad idea. That is a bad idea full of bad manners.

When Old Coyote hears this bad idea, she starts to laugh. Who would buy Indians, she says, and she laughs some more. She laughs so hard, she has to hold her nose on her face with both her hands.

But while that Old Coyote is laughing, Christopher Columbus grabs a bunch of Indian men and Indian women and Indian children and locks them up in his ships.

When Old Coyote stops laughing and looks around, she sees that some of the Indians are missing. Hey, she says, where are those Indians? Where are my friends?

I'm going to sell them in Spain, says Christopher Columbus. Somebody has to pay for this trip. Sailing over the ocean blue isn't cheap, you know.

But Old Coyote still thinks that Christopher Columbus is playing a trick. She thinks it is a joke. That is a good joke, she says, trying to make me think that you are going to sell my friends. And she starts to laugh again.

Grab some more Indians, says Christopher Columbus.

When Old Coyote sees Christopher Columbus grab some more Indians, she laughs even harder. What a good joke, she says. And she laughs some more. She does this four times and when she is done laughing, all the Indians are gone. And Christopher Columbus is gone and Christopher Columbus's friends are gone, too.

Wait a minute, says Old Coyote. What happened to my friends? Where are my Indians? You got to bring them back. Who's going to play ball with me?

But Christopher Columbus didn't bring the Indians back and Old Coyote was real sorry she thought him up. She tried to take him back. But, you know, once you think things like that, you can't take them back. So you have to be careful what you think.

So. That's the end of the story.

Boy, says Coyote. That is one sad story.

Yes, I says. It's sad alright. And things don't get any better, I can tell you that.

What a very sad story, says Coyote. Poor Old Coyote didn't have anyone to play ball with. That one must have been lonely. And Coyote begins to cry.

Stop crying, I says. Old Coyote is fine. Some blue jays come along after that and they play ball with her.

Oh, good, says Coyote. But what happened to the Indians? There was nothing in that red history book about Christopher Columbus and the Indians.

Christopher Columbus sold the Indians, I says, and that one became rich and famous.

Oh, good, says Coyote. I love a happy ending. And that one blows her party whistle and that one shakes her party rattle and that one puts her party hat back on her head. I better get going, she says, I'm going to be late for the party.

Okay, I says. Just remember how that story goes. Don't go messing it up again. Have you got it straight, now?

You bet, says Coyote. But if Christopher Columbus didn't find America and he didn't find Indians, who found these things?

Those things were never lost, I says. Those things were always here. Those things are still here today.

By golly, I think you are right, says Coyote.

Don't be thinking, I says. This world has enough problems already without a bunch of Coyote thoughts with tails and scraggy fur running around bumping into each other.

Boy, that's the truth. I can tell you that.

—*Source: Thomas King*, One Good Story, That One *(HarperCollins Publishers Ltd., 1993), pp. 117-127.*

RECONNECT

1. Why was storytelling so important in traditional Aboriginal culture?

2. What common themes do Aboriginal writers employ in contemporary writing?

Contact to Confederation: from Allies to Wards of the State

FOCUS

This section will help you understand
  a. what happened when Aboriginal and non-Aboriginal cultures came into contact
  b. some of the important changes in the historical relationship between Aboriginal and non-Aboriginal peoples.

TIMELINE — Historic Milestones

1624	First written treaty between the French and Haudenosaunee (Iroquois) Confederacy.
1763	British win control of Canada; Royal Proclamation recognizes Aboriginal rights to land and self-government.
1784-88	First Nations support British during the American Revolutionary War and British government grants them reserve lands in the Grand River area.
1812-15	First Nations cooperate with Britain in War of 1812 against the United States.
1816	Métis force settlers to abandon first Red River settlement in Battle of Seven Oaks; Métis Nation emerges.
1829	Shawnadithit, last known member of the Beothuk First Nation, dies.
1850	Robinson-Superior and Robinson-Huron Treaties signed in what is now Ontario.
1850-54	Governor of the Vancouver Island Colony signs treaties with some Aboriginal people on Vancouver Island.
1869-70	Métis resist transfer of Rupert's Land to Canada; Manitoba Act acknowledges Métis rights and creates province of Manitoba.
1871-77	Treaties #1 to #7 signed on Prairies.
1876	Indian Act is passed establishing government policies of assimilation.
1884	Potlatch is banned but Aboriginal peoples continue these traditional ceremonies.
1895	Famous Mohawk poet Pauline Johnson (Tekahionwake) publishes her first volume of poems.
1907	Nisga'a Land Committee in British Columbia begins the long battle for recognition of land rights in that province.
1914-18	Aboriginal men enlist to fight in World War 1 though they do not have the full rights of Canadian citizens.
1919	Mohawk Fred Loft establishes League of Indians of Canada, the first attempt at a national voice for Aboriginal peoples.
1939-45	Over 3000 Aboriginal soldiers and nurses serve during World War II.
1960	Registered Indians gain the right to vote in federal elections.
1969	Government White Paper on Aboriginal policy is defeated; this victory stirs a surge in Aboriginal art and literature with publications such as Harold Cardinal's *Unjust Society* and Maria Campbell's *Halfbreed*.
1982	New Constitution, in the Charter of Rights and Freedoms, recognizes Aboriginal rights.
1990	Manitoba MLA Elijah Harper derails the Meech Lake Accord which ignored concerns of Aboriginal leaders in constitutional reforms.

Figure 12-1   In 1997, Ovide Mercredi, past leader of the Assembly of First Nations, protested the 500th anniversary celebrations of John Cabot's arrival in Newfoundland. The poster shows *Demasduwit*, one of the last Beothuks. The Beothuks died from disease and clashes with Europeans. By 1829, there was not one Beothuk left.

set. The English and French would wage war for control of North America for 150 years. Aboriginal peoples would be embroiled in that battle and its aftermath.

From Sovereign Allies...

Though there were clashes the earliest relations between Aboriginal peoples and Europeans were mainly friendly. They were allies and trading partners. Early European explorers and fur traders needed the cooperation of Aboriginal peoples. Aboriginal peoples helped Cartier's men survive their first winter in what is now Quebec in 1535. Without the key role Aboriginal peoples played, the fur trade would not have been profitable. European powers also realized that they needed the support of Aboriginal people in the struggle to win political control of North America. The English, for example, allied themselves with the Haudenosaunee (Iroquois) Confederacy against the French.

For their parts, Aboriginal peoples recognized the benefits the fur trade brought them, especially in new trade goods. In the power struggle between the English and French, they entered into alliances to protect their own territories. They signed treaties as agreements between **sovereign** nations.

In 1763, the fight between the British and French for control of Canada ended. In that year, Britain issued the Royal Proclamation outlining its plans for the new colony. The Royal Proclamation included some key terms affecting Aboriginal peoples. It acknowledged that Aboriginal peoples lived as nations which had a claim or title to their traditional lands. It also stated that only the British government (and not any individual settlers or other groups) could buy Aboriginal lands or sign treaties with Aboriginal peoples for lands. Recent court cases affecting Aboriginal rights to land in Canada still refer to this document.

Contact: Europeans Arrive

The year 1997 marked the 500th anniversary of John Cabot's arrival in Newfoundland. While there were celebrations on the East Coast, Aboriginal nations did not share the same sense of celebration. The long history of contact between Europeans and Aboriginal peoples have had a devastating impact on Aboriginal peoples.

The Vikings were among the earliest Europeans to reach North America. When they landed in Newfoundland around 1000 CE, they referred to the Aboriginal people they met as *skraelings* or "little wretches." This ethnocentric view of Aboriginal peoples as "backward" and "uncivilized" lasted well into the 20th century.

The Vikings did not establish permanent settlements in North America. The next main contact came almost 500 years later when European fishers reached the Grand Banks off Newfoundland. The English sent John Cabot to explore and claim land in 1497. In 1534, the French sent Jacques Cartier and later Samuel de Champlain. The pattern was

Figure 12-2   This famous painting shows Iroquoians providing Cartier and his men with boiled cedar bark to cure scurvy. Without the cure, the Europeans would not have survived the winter.

Though the Europeans saw Aboriginal peoples as vital participants in North America in the 1600s and 1700s, they tried to change Aboriginal customs and religious practices. For hundreds of years, Christian missionaries worked to assimilate and convert Aboriginal peoples to their ways. While many missionaries tried to completely change traditional cultures, others respected those cultures.

The conversion of some Aboriginal peoples divided Aboriginal communities. Christian converts wanted to move away from traditional beliefs and behaviours, while others respected the traditional ways. These divisions helped to undermine Aboriginal cultures. Today some Aboriginal people see Christian missionary work as an unwelcome interference in their lives, while many others are proud Christians.

... To Wards of the State

In the War of 1812, Aboriginal peoples were again allies of the British against the Americans. After that war, however, European and North American governments no longer needed the military support of Aboriginal peoples. In Ontario, rapid immigration after the American Revolutionary War meant great pressure for land. Settlers saw the Aboriginal peoples as obstacles to settlement. Starting in the 1830s, Canadian governments acquired Aboriginal peo-

Figure 12-3   Joseph Brant (Thayendanegea), a Mohawk, believed the British could help protect his people's lands from seizures by American settlers. During the American Revolutionary War, Brant fought with the British against the Americans. Following the war when British Loyalists were given land in what became Canada, Brant demanded the same for his people. His campaign was eventually successful. Over 3 million acres along the Grand River was purchased from the Mississaugas in southwestern Ontario. The Six Nations were given the land "to enjoy forever."

EyeWitness

The Ojibwa chief, Minweweh, who had fought with the French against the British expressed his view of his people as a sovereign nation.

"Although you have conquered the French, you have not conquered us. We are not your slaves. These lakes, these woods and mountains were left us by our ancestors. They are our inheritance, and we will part with them to none."

— Ojibwa Chief Minweweh quoted in *Attack at Michilimackinac 1763*, ed. David A. Armour (Macinac Island, Michigan: 1988), p. 25.

ples' lands to create **reserves**. In 1836, for example, the Lieutenant-Governor of Upper Canada Sir Francis Bond Head, believing Aboriginal peoples to be a "doomed race," suggested that all Aboriginal people in Ontario be shipped to Manitoulin Island where they could be protected.

Economic decline matched the political decline of Aboriginal peoples. The demand and supply for furs was no longer steady and the role of Aboriginal peoples in the fur trade was no longer secure. Many Aboriginal peoples could not keep up their traditional hunting and gathering lifestyles. Whether it was the beaver in the East, the buffalo on the Prairies or the otter and seal on the West Coast, the story was the same: the declining importance of hunting and trapping meant the end of Aboriginal economic power.

Disease also drastically reduced Aboriginal populations. They did not have immunities to such diseases as measles and smallpox. Thousands upon thousands died after exposure to infected Europeans.

By the time of Confederation in 1867, most Canadian politicians in the four provinces making up Canada—Quebec, Ontario, New Brunswick, and Nova Scotia—no longer believed it was necessary to consider the wishes of Aboriginal peoples. Aboriginal peoples were not included in the discussions that led to the creation of Canada. Under the Constitution of 1867, the federal government assumed responsibility for "Indians" and land reserved for "Indians." With the passage of the Indian Act in 1876, "Indians" were considered **wards** of the state. In other words, they were no longer considered independent, self-governing peoples. They were placed under the guardianship of the Canadian government which determined the rules by which they would live. They did not have the same rights as other Canadians.

By the 20th century, the effects of disease along with the social, economic and political disruption of their lives had demoralized many Aboriginal people. Despite these problems, Aboriginal peoples have continued to fight for their rights.

Figure 12-4 Before the arrival of the Europeans, Aboriginal populations in Canada have been estimated at somewhere between several hundred thousand and over a million. For hundreds of years, Aboriginal peoples outnumbered Europeans in North America. By the 1910s, however, their population bottomed out at just over 100 000. They had become a minority. Recently, however, Aboriginal populations have grown much more rapidly than the non-Aboriginal Canadian population. What factors led to the massive decline in the Aboriginal population and to its recent increase?

EyeWitness

Changing Attitudes Toward First Nations

This statement by Prime Minister John A. Macdonald in 1887 demonstrated the key shift in attitudes toward Aboriginal peoples after Confederation.

"The great aim of our legislation has been to do away with the tribal system and assimilate the Indian people in all respects with the other inhabitants of the Dominion as speedily as they are fit to change."

—Malcolm Montgomery, "The Six Nations Indians and the Macdonald Franchise."

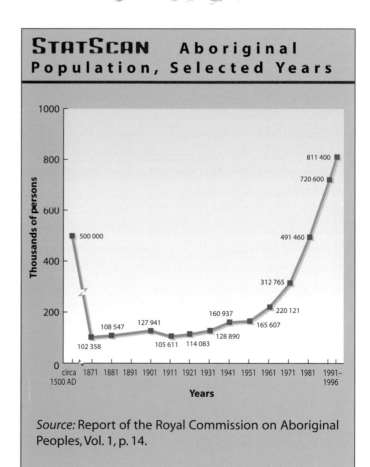

STATSCAN   Aboriginal Population, Selected Years

Source: Report of the Royal Commission on Aboriginal Peoples, Vol. 1, p. 14.

RECONNECT

1. Describe the relationship between Aboriginal peoples and Europeans/Canadians in each of the following periods: (a.) contact to 1815 and (b.) after 1815.

2. Outline four reasons for the political and economic decline of Aboriginal peoples.

FOCUS

This section will help you understand
- a. why governments in Canada and First Nations signed treaties
- b. the implications of these treaties today.

Why Were Treaties Signed?

The year 1869 was a significant one. In that year, the Canadian government bought Rupert's Land (which included all lands draining into Hudson Bay) from the Hudson's Bay Company. A vast new area of land was open for settlement. Between 1871 and 1929, a number of treaties were signed between Aboriginal nations and Canadian governments for these lands. What was the government's motivation in signing these treaties?

▶ Government officials feared the area was open to an American takeover. Prime Minister John A. Macdonald was determined to fill the area with settlers and secure Canada's claim.

▶ Following the terms set by the Royal Proclamation of 1763, agreements had to be made with Aboriginal peoples for their lands.

▶ In the United States, conflicts between Aboriginal nations and settlers had been bloody. In parts of Canada, there had already been unrest where settlers had moved into lands occupied by Aboriginal nations. As a result of these conflicts, the government signed the Robinson-Superior and the Robinson-Huron treaties covering the north shore of Lake Huron and Lake Superior in 1850.

▶ The government was determined to continue its policy of acting as guardian and gradually assimilating Aboriginal peoples. By creating reserves, lands set aside for Aboriginal peoples on which they would have hunting and fishing rights, Aboriginal peoples would be "protected." The government could also control their education and convert their way of life to farming.

What was the motivation of Aboriginal nations?

▶ Aboriginal peoples were not prepared to allow settlers to simply take possession of their lands. Their resistance put pressure on the Canadian government to negotiate.

▶ Aboriginal leaders such as Chief Crowfoot of the Siksika (Blackfoot) recognized that with the destruction of the buffalo herds, their way of life was collapsing. They needed assurances for their futures and new means of livelihood when they could no longer follow their traditional economies.

▶ As independent peoples and nations, Aboriginal leaders were prepared to negotiate with the officials of the Canadian government to protect their rights and their peoples or to fight for those rights. The first treaties guaranteed Aboriginal bands a reserve of their choice (land grants ranged from 160 to 640 acres per family of five), schools, annual payments of around $5 per person, livestock and farming tools, ammunition, seeds, and the right to hunt and fish in unoccupied land. Aboriginal peoples also insisted that the government provide education and instruction in farming.

The Treaties Today

Since the 1870s, many Aboriginal peoples have claimed that the treaties have been misinterpreted and that many terms have not been honoured. For example, the treaties did not include some oral promises made by government negotiators. Aboriginal peoples consider the oral promises binding and believe the treaties need to be reinterpreted in light of these oral promises. Elders in the Treaty 7 area, for example, say their oral history shows their ancestors believed they were signing an agreement of peace, friendship, and mutual support. In other words, they never intended to surrender their lands permanently to the government. They only intended to share their lands.

Areas Without Treaties

Many parts of the country are not covered by treaties. Today, Canadian governments are still signing agreements with Aboriginal people to extinguish Aboriginal

MapStudy   TREATY AREAS

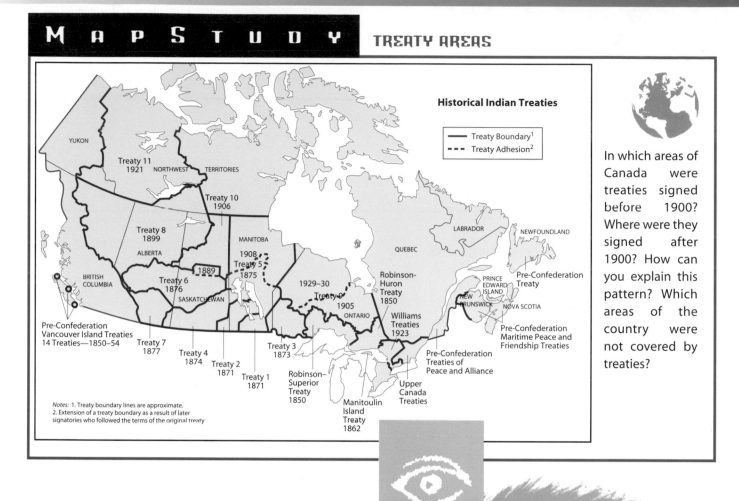

Historical Indian Treaties

——— Treaty Boundary[1]
- - - - Treaty Adhesion[2]

YUKON

Treaty 11
1921   NORTHWEST   TERRITORIES

Treaty 10
1906

Treaty 8
1899   MANITOBA

ALBERTA   1908
Treaty 5
1875   LABRADOR   NEWFOUNDLAND

BRITISH
COLUMBIA   1889   QUEBEC

Treaty 6
1876   1929–30
Treaty 9
1905   Robinson-
Huron
Treaty
1850   PRINCE
EDWARD
ISLAND   Pre-Confederation
Treaty

SASKATCHEWAN   ONTARIO   NEW
BRUNSWICK   NOVA SCOTIA

Williams
Treaties
1923

Pre-Confederation
Vancouver Island Treaties
14 Treaties—1850–54   Treaty 7
1877   Treaty 3
1873   Pre-Confederation
Maritime Peace and
Friendship Treaties

Treaty 4
1874   Robinson–
Superior
Treaty
1850   Pre-Confederation
Treaties of
Peace and Alliance

Treaty 2
1871   Upper
Canada
Treaties

Treaty 1
1871   Manitoulin
Island
Treaty
1862

Notes: 1. Treaty boundary lines are approximate.
2. Extension of a treaty boundary as a result of later
signatories who followed the terms of the original treaty

In which areas of Canada were treaties signed before 1900? Where were they signed after 1900? How can you explain this pattern? Which areas of the country were not covered by treaties?

title—the land rights Aboriginal people have based on their traditional occupation of land. In British Columbia, for example, the provincial government did not recognize Aboriginal title to lands after British Columbia joined Canada in 1871. Since that time, First Nations in the province have fought to have their Aboriginal title recognized.

Throughout Canada, First Nations have consistently argued that they have rights to their traditional lands. Recently, in three famous decisions—the Calder case of 1973, the Baker Lake case of 1979, and the Delgamuukw case of 1997—the Supreme Court of Canada has agreed with them. These cases establish the fact that in areas without treaties First Nations, because of their original habitation of the land, have rights to use the land that continue to this day.

EyeWitness

During the treaty making process of the 1870s, translation of the documents from English into the various Aboriginal languages was a problem. In some cases, translators were not sufficiently fluent in the relevant Aboriginal languages, and in others, some crucial English concepts such as *square mile, surrender, reserve* or **title** did not have equivalents in Aboriginal languages. In fact, equivalents of these words were only introduced into the Blackfoot language in the 1900s.

During the negotiation of Treaty 7 in 1877, official records of the negotiation process show that translators only relayed one-sixth of the full presentation of the Canadian negotiators. One Stoney Nation Elder, in describing the oral history of the negotiation, says that the Stoney people:

".... did not know in the White people's language what surrender meant — they did not talk about giving anything up... The White people [government] had placed this term in the treaty but the Natives did not know or were not aware of it, and thus did not talk about giving up anything."

— Stoney Nation Elder quoted in *The True Spirit and Original Intent of Treaty 7* (Kingston: McGill-Queen's University Press, 1996), p. 131.

RECONNECT

1. Why did the federal government sign treaties with First Nations?

2. Identify two reasons why some First Nations disagree with the government about the interpretation of treaties.

FOCUS

This section will help you understand
  a. the reasons for conflict between the Métis and the government of Canada in the 1800s
  b. the Resistance at Red River in 1870 and the 1885 Rebellion.

The Métis of the Prairies: An Emerging Nation

The Métis are people of mixed Aboriginal and European ancestry, descended from French and English fur traders and First Nations women. In the 1800s they lived throughout Canada, but a distinctive and important group was centred along the Red River south of present-day Winnipeg. This group spoke a language called Michif which blended French and Cree. Like their language, their unique way of life combined elements of Aboriginal and non-Aboriginal traditions: strip farms like those in Quebec, buffalo hunting, and trade. In the early 1800s, the Métis had begun to develop a sense of their distinct identity and to see themselves as a "new nation."

In 1811, the Hudson's Bay Company sold a large area of land in what is now Manitoba to Lord Selkirk who intended to establish a settlement in the Red River valley. When poor crops led the governor of the settlement to ban exports of **pemmican**, the major trade good of the Métis, they chose to demand their right to the land on which they lived and their right to hunt. In 1816, a group of Métis led by Cuthbert Grant won a key victory over a group of settlers at Seven Oaks. The Battle of Seven Oaks became a milestone in the formation of the Métis Nation. From then on, the Métis continued to demand their rights from the Hudson's Bay Company and successive British governments.

When the government of Canada bought Rupert's Land from the Hudson's Bay Company in 1869, neither group notified the Métis and other Aboriginal peoples living in the region. The Métis objected to not even being consulted and were concerned that settlers threatened their lands. They decided to resist. Louis Riel, well educated, fluent in English and French, and son of an important Métis leader, emerged to lead the cause.

Figure 14-1 The buffalo hunt was a central part of Métis culture. Hundreds of families would gather for the hunts. Captains were chosen in elections to lead the hunts and councils were held in the evenings to discuss and vote on rules. The captains, who included Cuthbert Grant and Gabriel Dumont, often became important military leaders of the Métis and used the tight organization and discipline of the hunt to their advantage in their military successes.

Figure 14-2 Comité National des Métis, 1869. Louis Riel is seated in the centre of the second row.

TIMELINE   Resistance at Red River, 1869-70

Canada purchases Rupert's Land from the Hudson's Bay Company.

Canadian government surveyors ignore the traditional Métis strip farms and survey plots in squares. Métis block William McDougall, Canada's official representative, from entering the region.

Nov. 1869 Riel and Métis capture Fort Garry, and create the Comité National des Métis to oversee the region.

Dec. 1869 Protestant immigrants from Ontario in the colony violently resist the Métis government. Riel arrests the protesters.

Feb. 1870 List of rights and demands from Red River settlers includes insistence that Manitoba become a province of Canada with equal use of French and English, representation in the Canadian Parliament, and protection for Métis lands.

Mar. 1870 Thomas Scott, a protestor under arrest by Riel's government, is executed. There is an outcry in Ontario against Riel's actions but support for him in French-speaking Quebec.

May 1870 Province of Manitoba is created; the government acknowledges Métis title to occupied lands and grants them more land.

Aug. 1870 New lieutenant-governor and military move into the region; fearing a reaction to Scott's execution, Riel flees to the United States.

The Rebellion of 1885

After 1870, the Métis received coupons from the federal government, called scrip, which could be used to purchase land. But with increasing immigration from eastern Canada, many Métis sold their land or scrip and moved further west where they could carry on their traditional lifestyle. During the 1870s, the Métis repeatedly asked the federal government for recognition of their land holdings in Alberta and Saskatchewan. The government ignored their requests.

In 1885, the buffalo had been hunted almost to extinction and the Métis in Saskatchewan were facing starvation. They decided to act. They called Riel back from his exile in the United States and declared their independence from Canada. Under the military leadership of Gabriel Dumont, the Métis gathered their forces and asked other Aboriginal peoples on the Prairies to join them.

The situation for many Aboriginal peoples was dire. Food shortages were severe and rations from the government were not enough. Government agents and farm instructors had little knowledge of Aboriginal peoples and little sympathy for them.

Some attempted to manipulate the people by cutting the food aid guaranteed in treaties. Still, most chiefs wanted to avoid conflict. Crowfoot and Piapot understood how disastrous the "Indian wars" in the United States had been for Aboriginal people living there. But some First Nations did join the Métis. Chiefs Poundmaker and Big Bear were unable to stop their followers from fighting the settlers and disobeying the government.

During the Rebellion of 1885 after some early successes, the First Nations and the Métis were defeated in a few months. The federal government imprisoned Poundmaker and Big Bear and a jury convicted Riel of treason. Despite national and international pleas for a pardon, the government hanged Riel a few months after the rebellion ended.

Since then, the Métis have tried to have Louis Riel **exonerated**. In 1998, the federal government announced it was willing "to look for ways...of reflecting Louis Riel's proper place in Canadian history." Groups representing the Métis rejected this move, arguing that the reforms Riel fought for were not being addressed.

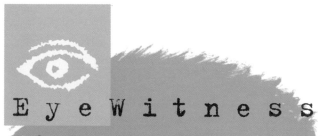

EyeWitness

Broken Treaty Promises

Cree Chief Piapot was one of those frustrated by the fact that the government was not honouring its treaty promises while his people were facing starvation.

"In order to become sole masters of our land they relegated us to small reservations as big as my hand and make us long promises, as long as my arm; but the next year the promises were shorter and got shorter every year until now they are the length of my finger, and they keep only half of that."

—Chief Piapot of the Cree (1828-1908) quoted in *First People, First Voices*, Regina: Saskatchewan Archives Board.

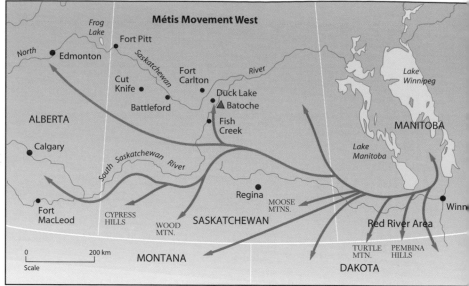

Figure 14-3   After 1870, many Métis moved west into what is now southern Saskatchewan and Alberta.

Figure 14-4   The battle at Batoche in May 1885 was a decisive one during the Rebellion. A force of 850 under General Middleton battled about 350 Métis. The Canadian forces had the advantage of Gatling guns, an early machine gun. After three days, the Métis ran out of ammunition. Riel surrendered. Total lives lost in the rebellion: 53 non-Aboriginals killed, 118 wounded; approximately 35 First Nations and Métis people killed.

Figure 14-5   Riel was tried in Regina on a charge of treason. His jury was made up of six English-speaking Protestants. Riel was a French-speaking Roman Catholic and his supporters feared he would not get a fair trial. Riel's lawyers tried to argue that Riel was insane and was not responsible for his actions during the rebellion, but Riel refused to accept this defence.

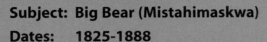

BIOGRAPHY

Figure 14-6 Big Bear (Mistahimaskwa).

Subject: Big Bear (Mistahimaskwa)

Dates: 1825-1888

Most Notable Accomplishment: As a chief of the Plains Cree in the 1870s, Big Bear continually worked to gain better terms for his people from the Canadian government as the buffalo were disappearing from the Plains.

Thumbnail Sketch: By 1870, Big Bear had emerged as an influential chief among the Plains Cree. Faced with the disappearance of the buffalo and an increasing number of settlers, Big Bear knew his people's way of life was in danger. He was not convinced, however, that treaties were the answer. Big Bear refused to sign Treaty 6 in 1876 because he believed the treaty conditions would lead to perpetual poverty and destroy his people's way of life. He was also not prepared to submit his people to Canadian laws.

When the Rebellion of 1885 broke out, Big Bear did not want to become involved in violence. Along with Chiefs Piapot and Little Pine, he worked to unite various bands to present a stronger front in their dealings with the government. In the summer of 1884, he helped to organize a council of 12 band leaders at Duck Lake to push for revisions to the treaties and to protest the government's poor record in honouring its treaty promises.

As food shortages became more and more severe, however, Big Bear could not control his younger war chiefs who were determined to fight. They took provisions from stores at Frog Lake. Nine people were killed. Big Bear's intervention saved the Hudson's Bay Company representative, and the women and children. Pursued by a Canadian force, he eventually surrendered on July 2, 1885.

CROSSFIRE

Should Louis Riel be recognized as a hero and a Father of Confederation for his role in establishing the province of Manitoba?

Arguments For

While we were young, at least in the public schools, they produced a warped version of the facts and basically created Riel as a traitor. It is now recognized by the government that the lands here did belong to the Aboriginal people.
—Leo Teillet, great grand-nephew of Louis Riel quoted in "Riel is hero, not traitor, family says," *Ottawa Citizen*, April 12, 1998, p. A5.

Without his intervention, the federal government of the time would have turned the present western provinces into territories run by governors appointed by Ottawa.
—Suzanne Tremblay, Bloc Québécois MP who put forward a bill to revoke the conviction against Riel in 1996.

Arguments Against

Riel's act of establishing a "provisional government" was simple rebellion. Without the legal force of duly constituted government, the killing of Thomas Scott was illegal: It was murder.
—Editorial, "Riel, Scott and History," *Ottawa Citizen*, Feb. 1, 1998.

Why was Riel hanged? His judge had little alternative: Grievances did not give anyone the right to organize and lead a rebellion in which more than a hundred died.
—Canadian historian Desmond Morton, quoted in "Reconfiguring Riel," *Ottawa Citizen,* Jan. 22,1998.

RECONNECT

1. List two reasons why the Métis were dissatisfied with the government of Canada in 1869 and in 1885.

2. Some people consider Louis Riel a traitor and some consider him a hero. Provide two facts that could be used to support each of these opinions.

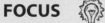

FOCUS

This section will help you understand
a. the major terms of the Indian Act and their effects
b. how the Act has been changed over its history.

A Controversial Act

In 1876, the Canadian government passed the Indian Act. Throughout its history, the Act has sparked controversy. Though meant as a temporary measure, it has been changed many times and still affects the lives of Aboriginal peoples today.

In 1876, the Indian Act defined who was an "Indian" under the law and outlined what "Indians" could and could not do. It was a clear statement of the federal government's policy to act as guardians over Aboriginal peoples, giving them "protection" but with the ultimate goal of assimilating them. As Duncan Campbell Scott, Deputy Superintendent of Indian Affairs from 1913 to 1932 stated: "The happiest future for the Indian race is absorption into the general population, and this is the object of the policy of our government. The great forces of intermarriage and education will finally overcome the lingering traces of native custom and tradition."

Agents of the Department of Indian Affairs enforced the Act for most of its history and had almost dictatorial control over many aspects of Aboriginal peoples' lives.

This section focuses on Indian status and the right to vote. In the following sections you will see how the Indian Act was used in banning traditional practices of Aboriginal peoples, controlling their education, governing their reserve lands, and restricting their political actions.

Indian Status and Enfranchisement

Under the Indian Act," Indians" did not have the full rights of Canadian citizens. For example, they did not have the right to vote. The federal government expected Aboriginal peoples to eventually give up their status and become full citizens. To this end, it introduced a policy of **enfranchisement**. In one sense, enfranchisement means gaining the right to vote, but it also became a term that referred to giving up or losing Indian status since the only way "Indians" could gain the right to vote was if they gave up their status.

Status Indians considered "of good character" who voluntarily gave up their Indian status were given individual ownership of a plot of land on a reserve, the right to buy and consume alcohol, and the right to vote. Very few Aboriginal people, however, wanted to give up their status (from 1876 to 1918, only 102 Indians were enfranchised). To many, it meant giving up their identity.

For a brief time in the 1920s, the federal government tried to enfranchise Indian veterans of World War I against their will. Any Indians who received university degrees also automatically had to give up their status, as did any woman who married a non-Aboriginal man. The over 3000 Aboriginal soldiers who fought with the Canadian forces during World War II were also expected to enfranchise. When they returned from the war, however, they did not receive the right to vote or own land, and they were not paid veteran's pension. It was not until 1960 that Registered Indians received the right to vote in Canadian elections without having to give up their status.

Figure 15-1 Aboriginal veterans of World War I. The federal government tried to enfranchise the veterans against their will after the war.

CaseStudy

WOMEN WIN BATTLE AGAINST DISCRIMINATION IN THE INDIAN ACT

Amongst the controversial issues surrounding the Indian Act, one major flashpoint was women's rights. Under the Indian Act, if an Aboriginal woman married a Non-Status Indian or non-Aboriginal man, she lost her Indian status. Her children also had no rights to status. On the other hand, an Aboriginal man kept his status no matter whom he married. The Indian Act determined status through **patrilineal** lines (through the father's family), even though some First Nations such as the Mohawks and Haida traditionally defined their family lineage through **matrilineal** lines.

For years, Aboriginal women raised their voices against this discrimination in the Act. In 1938 Mary Two-Axe Earley, a Mohawk woman born on the Kahnawake Reserve in Quebec, married a non-Aboriginal man. She automatically lost her Indian status and no longer had the right to go back and live on the reserve as long as she remained married. In 1966, the band refused to allow another woman who had lost her status to be buried on the reserve with her people. This event sparked Two-Axe Earley to found Equal Rights for Indian Women, an organization that protested for the rights of Aboriginal women.

The battle became more heated in the 1970s when it hit the courts. Jeanette Courbiere, an Ojibwa woman from Manitoulin Island, lost her status when she married a non-Aboriginal man, David Lavell in 1970. She decided to take her case to court, but lost. The following year, she won in an appeal to the federal court. Not all Aboriginal bands supported her cause or recognized the decisions of the Canadian courts. They saw the court decision as interference in their affairs and appealed to the Supreme Court of Canada. The Supreme Court ruled, by a slim majority, that the Indian Act did not discriminate against Jeanette Lavell because it treated all Indian women in the same way.

The key battle was won in 1981. Sandra Lovelace, a Maliseet from the Tobique Reserve in New Brunswick, took her complaint beyond the Canadian courts to the Human Rights Committee of the United Nations. The Committee ruled that the Indian Act violated human rights. The Indian Act, however, was not officially changed until 1985. Mary Two-Axe Earley was the first Aboriginal woman to have her status restored.

People who had lost status through enfranchisement or by obtaining a university degree also regained their status. Since 1985, over 100 000 people have won back their status. Bands were given the right to determine their own membership. As a result, not all Status or Registered Indians belong to a band today.

Figure 15-2 The National Action Committe on the Status of Women declared October 22, 1973 a national day of mourning for the Canadian Bill of Rights to draw attention to the Supreme Court of Canada's decision in the Lavell case.

Figure 15-3 Mary Two-Axe Earley was recognized with an Aboriginal Achievement Award in 1996 for her work in women's rights.

RECONNECT

1. What specific evidence is there that the Indian Act is being slowly changed and improved?

2. In your opinion, should the Indian Act be repealed?

FOCUS

This section will help you understand
  a. why the federal government banned certain cultural practices of Aboriginal peoples
  b. how Aboriginal peoples reacted to the bans.

Why Were Bans Introduced?

In the late 19th and early 20th centuries, the thrust of government policies toward Aboriginal peoples was clear. The federal government wanted Aboriginal peoples to abandon their traditional beliefs and adopt Christian and "democratic" values. But many Aboriginal peoples were not prepared to give up beliefs and practices that had been ingrained in their cultural lives for thousands of years. As Indian agents continually reported slow progress, government regulations became increasingly **coercive**. In some cases, bans were placed on traditional activities of some Aboriginal peoples.

Banning the Potlatch

The potlatch was an important cultural and spiritual practice among Aboriginal peoples on the Pacific northwest coast. Chiefs used potlatches to

Figure 16-1 Hudson's Bay Company blankets, eulachon oil (oil made from the eulachon fish), canoes and coppers (flat copper plaques) were the main objects distributed at potlatches although flour and manufactured items were also given away.

name children, to announce an important marriage, to transfer titles and privileges from father to son, and to mourn the dead. The chief and his family enhanced their honour and status at the potlatch by reciting their family history and by giving away valuable gifts. This ceremony showed their wealth, and guests who accepted the goods showed they agreed to the honours being claimed. The potlatch also served an economic function by redistributing wealth.

But some missionaries, Aboriginal Christians, and Hudson's Bay Company traders complained that the potlatch ceremony encouraged non-Christian beliefs and distracted Aboriginal people from "productive work." As trade goods had become more available and valuable, potlatches had been held on a grander scale and sometimes were fiercely competitive. In some cases, large quantities of goods were ceremoniously destroyed. Opponents of the ceremony seized on these cases as proof that the potlatch was destructive and "backward," leading the people into poverty. The federal government agreed. In 1884, participation in a potlatch was made an offence with a penalty of up to six months in jail.

People continued to practise the potlatch "underground" avoiding government officials. At first, the government rarely enforced the ban. But in the 1920s, pressure mounted for a crackdown. Officials arrested many potlatch participants and forced Aboriginal peoples on the West Coast to surrender ceremonial and sacred objects. The ban on the potlatch was not lifted until 1951.

Banning the Traditional Council of the Six Nations

In the early years of this century, pressures from government and settlers led the Six Nations into a number of controversial land deals and left the people demoralized and divided. In 1908, a group of Six Nations reformers dissatisfied with the traditional council sought more power on the reserve. They petitioned the federal government to replace the traditional council with an elected council. The Indian Act of 1876 required elected band councils, but the government had tolerated the traditional council (whose members were selected by clan mothers).

In the early 1920s, the traditional council under Chief Deskaheh prevailed over the reformers. Deskaheh was determined to fight against assimilation and Canadian government interference in Six Nations affairs. The council decided to seek international recognition of the Six Nations as an independent nation equal to the other nations of the world. Deskaheh put his argument before the Supreme Court of Canada, the British government, the King of England, and the League of Nations.

Deskaheh met with little success, but the federal government resented these actions. It blocked all attempts by the Six Nations to gain international attention. In an escalating conflict, the government first posted an RCMP detachment on the reserve in

Figure 16-2 This photo, dating from the early 1870s, shows chiefs from the traditional council on the Six Nations Reserve reading wampum belts. Though an elected council is the official representative of the Six Nations today, the traditional council continues to operate.

1923. Then, in 1924, the police expelled the traditional council and seized the sacred wampum belts used to sanction its meetings. An elected council became the official representative of the Six Nations and remains so to this day.

CROSSFIRE

In what way are the following statements: a) similar and b) different? Do you think that the potlatch should have been banned?

We will dance when our laws command us to dance, we will feast when our hearts desire to feast. Do we ask the white man, "do as the Indian does"? No, we do not. Why then do you ask us, "do as the white man does"?

It is a strict law that bids us dance. It is a strict law that bids us distribute our property among our friends and neighbours. It is a good law. Let the white man observe his law, we shall observe ours.

—Kwakwa̱ka'wakw chief, 1896, quoted in Peter Nabokov ed., *Aboriginal American Testimony: A Chronicle of Indian-white Relations from Prophecy to the Present, 1492-1992.*

The giving away of gifts on a lavish scale was one of the most prominent features of the potlatch. Before the advent of the White man this plan undoubtedly served a useful purpose and was adequate to the needs of the people. Obviously, however, with the introduction of the new money system of economics, engagement of the Indians as wage earners in industry, the effects of the potlatch, if the practice were unchecked, would be disastrous.

—Duncan Campbell Scott, Deputy Superintendent of the Department of Indian Affairs, 1931 quoted in *The Indian: Assimilation, Integration, or Separation?*

RECONNECT

1. Identify the purposes of the potlatch in West Coast First Nations culture.

2. Why did the Canadian government seek to ban the potlatch and traditional First Nations governments?

FOCUS

This section will help you understand
a. the nature and purpose of residential schools
b. the long-term impact of these schools on Aboriginal peoples.

> At the Indian residential school, we were not allowed to speak our language; we weren't allowed to dance, sing because they told us it was evil. It was evil for us to practise any of our cultural ways.
> —Kamloops Indian Residential School student.

The Purpose of Residential Schools

By the Indian Act, the federal government had responsibility for providing educational services to Aboriginal children. Beginning in the mid 1800s, the government began establishing what would become the residential school system. The schools were funded by the government but were operated by the Catholic, Anglican, Presbyterian, and United churches. By 1931, the churches were operating 80 residential schools across the country, as well as day schools on some reserves.

For the federal government, the schools were another cornerstone in its policy of assimilating Aboriginal peoples into mainstream society. Aboriginal children were removed from their homes and lived in these residential schools. Officials believed that the best way to assimilate the children was to separate them from their families, communities, and culture. The schools were also meant to promote economic **self-sufficiency** by teaching Aboriginal children to become farmers and labourers.

The goal of missionaries who taught at the schools was to convert the children to Christianity. Children were often severely punished for practising traditional spiritual beliefs. Aboriginal peoples sent their children to the schools because they wanted them to receive an education. Many parents believed their children needed the skills to participate in the new economy and society.

Life at the schools was often harsh and rules were strict. Much of the day was spent in Christian religious instruction, learning English or French, doing chores such as laundry and kitchen work,

Figure 17-1 These photographs from 1896 show Thomas Moore, a young Aboriginal boy, before he attended a residential school in Regina and after he had been at the school for some time. Officials and missionaries often used photographs like these to show the radical change brought about by the "benefits" of the residential schools.

and learning some practical skills. Boys were taught farming and some trade skills such as carpentry and blacksmithing. Girls learned household skills such as sewing and cooking. The schools typically spent less than two hours per day on academic subjects. Many students felt the system left them ill-prepared for life outside the schools.

Lasting Impacts

For the most part, students received a poor education at residential schools. In 1945, for example, few students completed grade 9 and over 40% of the teaching staff had no professional training. Many children died of illnesses or caught diseases such as tuberculosis which destroyed their health. In an environment where they were often poorly fed and ill-treated, students did not learn well. Many parents began withdrawing their children from the schools and refusing to participate in the system. The schools were not phased out, however, until the 1960s.

Residential schools have had a devastating long-term effect on Aboriginal people and their communities. The schools broke the connection between children and their parents and culture. Many children, unable to reconnect to their family and culture after the enforced isolation and anti-Aboriginal instruction, rejected their past. Others suffered from the effects of physical, sexual, and psychological

Figure 17-2 This photo of a dining room in a residential school reflects the strict supervision and table manners. Boys and girls were separated.

abuse. In 1996, the Report of the Royal Commission on Aboriginal peoples pointed to residential schools as a major factor in the high rates of substance abuse, suicide, and family problems among Aboriginal peoples. On the other hand, many students have begun the healing process or have moved on to lead successful and healthy lives.

EyeWitness

These quotations, from students at the Kamloops Indian Residential School in British Columbia 1907 to 1963, describe their feelings and experiences.

Before I left [home], I was full of confidence; I could do everything that was needed to be done at home. ...But when I arrived here all that left me. I felt so helpless. The Shuswap language was no use to me ... the supervisors couldn't understand.

I was punished quite a bit because I spoke my language...I was put in a corner and punished and sometimes, I was just given bread and water...Or they'd try to embarrass us and they'd put us in front of the whole class.

...Leona came and we were all talking Shuswap...She said to us, "You're never to get caught talking your language...You'll get whipped; you'll really get punished"...So we were careful after that not to be caught speaking...When we were way out there, we'd talk together in our language.

Something I remember is that I was always hungry. I lost weight there. I gained ten to twelve pounds in two months at home.

They censored all our letters...They would make a big speech if we complained about food in a letter. There wasn't very many that complained...'cause we knew it wouldn't get out anyway.

—Celia Haig-Brown, *Resistance and Renewal: Surviving the Indian Residential School* (Vancouver: Tillacum Library, 1988).

RECONNECT

1. Identify ways in which residential schools differ from your school.

2. List ways residential schools encouraged or forced students to lose their Aboriginal identity.

3. Explain in a paragraph how residential schools caused social problems in Aboriginal communities.

FOCUS 💡

This section will help you understand
  a. how and why traditional economic activities of Aboriginal peoples changed in the 20th century
  b. how Aboriginal peoples attempted to find new sources of livelihood.

The Decline of the Fur Trade

For over 300 years the fur trade was the driving force in the economic life of Aboriginal peoples. At the turn of the 20th century, most Aboriginal peoples, especially in the western provinces and the North, made their livings by hunting, trapping, and fishing. By the middle of the century, however, the fur trade had declined drastically. Aboriginal peoples could no longer depend on it for an income, nor could they continue their traditional ways of life.

A number of factors contributed to the decline of the fur trade and the difficult economic conditions Aboriginal peoples faced:

▶ The fur trade encouraged trappers to specialize in a limited number of fur-bearing animals; this often led to overtrapping and eventually a drastic decline in the number of available animals.

▶ The fur trade was further affected by bans on hunting endangered species and on the seal hunt, as well as changing fashions; fur coats and other fur clothing became less fashionable and more controversial.

▶ Government programs such as family allowance, which was introduced after World War II and required children to attend school, meant that families could no longer move with the seasons to follow game; Aboriginal families had to stay close to schools on reserves and remote reserves often had few economic possibilities.

▶ Pollution and conflicts over fishing rights also undermined fishing as a source of income. At the Grassy Narrows Reserve in Ontario, for example, mercury pollution of local waterways in the 1970s meant people could no longer engage in commercial fishing.

▶ Few types of work were available on reserves when traditional work was no longer possible. During the 1920s and 1930s, for example, the Inuit and northern Cree suffered desperate poverty when hunting and fur trapping could no longer provide them with a livelihood. In remote areas, there were few other types of employment and Aboriginal people often became dependent on credit or government assistance.

The Struggle for New Sources of Income

At the turn of the century, Aboriginal peoples were faced with trying to find new sources of livelihood. Many Aboriginal peoples had to turn to government assistance for help or look for whatever work they could find off the reserves. Some sold their arts and crafts such as baskets and blankets. On the West Coast, many found jobs in the commercial fishery. On the Prairies, many took up farming and ranching after the near extinction of the buffalo. The Department of Indian Affairs tried to help with the transition to farming, but often provided misguided advice. As a result, few Aboriginal people

Figure 18-1 The fur trade was at the centre of economic life for most Aboriginal people until the early 20th century.

became successful farmers. Many members of the Blood, Siksika, and Peigan First Nations in Alberta, however, became successful ranchers winning prizes as far away as Chicago in the 1920s. Some others, such as the Mohawk high steelworkers, also made the successful transition to skilled wage work. For most, however, economic conditions were extremely bad and their needs were often ignored.

The Road to Change

The economic boom after World War II through to the 1960s focused on the development of new resource industries (mining, logging, hydroelectric power, and so on) in lands often occupied or claimed by Aboriginal people. Sometimes Aboriginal people found work in these industries but there were no long-term economic benefits. The work was often low-wage unskilled labour and bands received no shares of the proceeds from the mines or forests on lands they considered theirs. Some bands managed to develop successful businesses, but real change did not begin until the 1970s with the settlement of lands claims such as the James Bay Agreement. Recent land agreements have typically included provisions for the establishment of Aboriginal businesses and gradually, success stories are becoming more numerous.

CaseStudy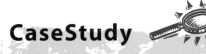

MOHAWK STEELWORKERS

In 1886, the Canadian Pacific Railway Company wanted to build a bridge across the St. Lawrence River near Montreal. The south end of the bridge would fall in Mohawk territory on the Kahnawake Reserve. To get permission to build the bridge, the company had to agree to hire people from the reserve. Their work on this bridge established the reputation of the Mohawk workers as skilled and expert bridge-builders. They took pride in mastering the profession and the wages were good. As their reputation spread, they were hired to build bridges and skyscrapers across Canada and the United States.

The work was often dangerous. In the early years of the century, there were no safety regulations and many men died in falls. In the worst disaster, 96 men were killed (33 of them Mohawks) when the Quebec Bridge collapsed into the St. Lawrence River in 1907. An iron cross was erected on the Kahnawake Reserve as a memorial to the dead workers. In the 1920s, many Mohawks went to work in New York City, attracted by the building boom. They were involved in the construction of such landmarks as the Empire State and Chrysler Buildings. Through the following decades, other Iroquois became involved in the trade and their work on major projects continued. In 1941, many participated in the completion of the Rainbow Bridge over Niagara Falls. Today, descendants of these workers continue the tradition. Many are highly successful and respected in the construction trade.

Figure 18-2 This painting by artist Arnold Jacobs is a tribute to the many Aboriginal workers, including his brother-in-law, who have been killed in accidents on high-steel building construction projects. The eagle in the painting celebrates the freedom the workers feel high above the cities and without walls.

RECONNECT

1. Provide three reasons why the fur trade has become unprofitable for many Aboriginal people.

2. What problems have Aboriginal people encountered when seeking non-traditional work?

3. What evidence is there that Aboriginal people can find economic success in Canada?

FOCUS

This section will help you understand
   a. why the federal government relocated some Aboriginal people
   b. the lasting impacts of these relocations.

The Pressure for Relocation

From the 1940s to the 1960s, towns and suburbs were growing rapidly in Canada and economic development was in full swing. During this period, the federal government relocated a number of Aboriginal peoples from their traditional lands. The main reasons for the relocations from the government's point of view were to improve economic conditions for Aboriginal people, to free land for development, and to make the administration of Aboriginal populations easier. Aboriginal people, however, rarely if ever had input into the decisions to relocate. Many found the adjustment to the new locations difficult and promises of better conditions, jobs, and housing were often not fulfilled. Sometimes families were split up and even those who went back to their original homes found their lives disrupted.

The Relocation of the Mi'kmaq in Nova Scotia

In the 1940s, for example, the Department of Indian Affairs decided to move all the Mi'kmaqs living throughout Nova Scotia onto two reserves, Eskasoni and Shubenacadie. The Mi'kmaqs had never signed land treaties with Canadian governments. Most lived in about 40 communities scattered throughout Nova Scotia. The government wanted to relocate the Mi'kmaqs to reduce the cost of delivering government services such as schools, health centres, and assistance payments.

To encourage the Mi'kmaqs to move, the government promised them better farms and schools and new jobs at the two new reserves. In some cases, officials threatened to end services at the old reserves. When the people arrived at the new reserves, they found the housing inadequate and the opportunities for jobs and better economic conditions wanting. Many decided to return to their original reserves. As a result, the government discontinued the program in 1949. Well into the 1980s, however, the Eskasoni and Shubenacadie Reserves were overcrowded and rates of substance abuse and suicide were high.

Figure 19-1 Housing conditions on the Eskasoni Reserve, Cape Breton Island, in the 1940s were poor.

E y e W i t n e s s

A Mi'kmaq woman explains why she and her family moved to Eskasoni and then moved back to their home reserve.

[W]e went to Eskasoni because we thought we had to. A man from Indian Affairs told us there would be no more school at our reserve, no medical services and no relief payments. He said that people who didn't move to Eskasoni wouldn't even be counted as Mi'kmaqs any more... None of this turned out to be true as we found out later.

Once the new houses were built, there were no jobs. The farm plot we were supposed to have was too far from our house. The soil was poor...

We were all so glad to leave Eskasoni that we didn't care that we might have no way to get our old farm going again.

—quoted in Robert M. Leavitt, *The Mi'kmacs,* (Toronto: Fitzhenry and Whiteside Ltd., 1985), pp. 51-52.

CaseStudy

HIGH ARCTIC RELOCATION IN THE 1950s

One of the most publicized cases of relocation occurred in the 1950s when the federal government moved Inuit groups in the North. In 1953, the government relocated several families of Inuit from Inukjuak, in northern Quebec, to Ellesmere and Cornwallis Islands in the High Arctic. The government stated the relocation was essential because of poor economic conditions at Inukjuak. The population had grown too large to live off the land, game was scarce, and it was feared the people may become dependent on government assistance. The government promised that the new areas had good hunting and better economic opportunities. Families were told they could return home after two years if they did not like the new areas.

The environment in the High Arctic was much different from what the Inukjuak families were used to. As a result they needed to learn to hunt different animals. They also faced a much shorter summer (six weeks compared to three and-a-half months in northern Quebec) and a long winter of complete darkness. From Inukjuak which had a school, nursing station, and weather and radio stations, they went to a desolate and uninhabited area. Several Inuit families from Pond Inlet on Baffin Island were brought in to help the Inukjuak families make the adjustment to the new locations. Cultural differences between the two groups, however, made cooperation difficult. Families had also been split up onto two different ships and sent to different locations. When some families asked to go home, their requests were refused. Many returned at their own expense in the 1970s and 1980s.

The Inuit claim the main reason for the relocation was because the government wanted to protect the Arctic islands from international claims during the **Cold War**. Human habitation was needed to establish Canadian sovereignty and so the Inuit were moved there. The Inuit believe they were not fully informed of the conditions and that their basic human needs were not met in the new locations. Though the government still maintained that the move was to improve economic conditions and that the people went willingly, it agreed in 1988 to pay $250 000 to cover the moving costs of those who returned to their original homes. In 1992, following a Canadian Human Rights Commission Report, the government announced it was willing to listen to Inuit concerns, acknowledged the emotional and physical hardship the people experienced, but offered no further compensation payments. Organizations such as the Inuit Tapirisat of Canada continue to press for an apology and for compensation.

Figure 19-3 What view of the Inuit relocation does this cartoon by Anthony Jenkins in *The Globe and Mail* present? How does the cartoon reflect the political and social climate of the time?

Figure 19-2 This map shows the relocation of the Inukjuak Inuit to Resolute Bay and Grise Ford in the High Arctic above the Arctic Circle. The move put the families a great distance from their original homes and in a very different environment.

Legend
Route of the Relocation–Inukjuak to Grise Fiord and Resolute Bay, 1953.

RECONNECT

1. List three ways in which the relocation of the Mi'kmaqs and the Inuit of Inukjuak were similar.

2. Provide two reasons why the government relocated Aboriginal peoples. Give an example of each.

FOCUS 💡

This section will help you understand
  a. how Aboriginal peoples tried to change government policies from 1900 to 1960
  b. why Aboriginal peoples undertook political action.

Early Political Activism

Early in the 20th century, Aboriginal peoples began to take political action to resist government policies of assimilation and interference. Aboriginal peoples in British Columbia were among the first to turn to political activism. The situation in British Columbia was unique. Only a few treaties had been signed in the province and after joining Confederation, the government refused to acknowledge Aboriginal title to land. Instead the government created a number of reserves which were much smaller than those on the Prairies.

In 1916, a provincial committee recommended reducing the number of reserves further by adding land to some and eliminating land from others. This was a call to action for Aboriginal peoples. Spearheaded by Reverend Peter Kelly (a Haida) and Squamish Chief Andrew Paull, the Allied Tribes of British Columbia was formed to fight for land claims. The Allied Tribes continued the battle for over 10 years, but with limited success. In 1927, the federal government decided that Aboriginal peoples "had not established any claim to the lands of British Columbia based on Aboriginal or other title." The government also changed the Indian Act, making it illegal for Aboriginal peoples to raise funds for land claims and restricting their rights to form political organizations. In the face of these restrictions, the Allied Tribes collapsed.

In 1931, the newly created Native Brotherhood of British Columbia continued the fight for recognition of Aboriginal title. It was not until the early 1990s, however, that the federal and provincial governments recognized Aboriginal title in British Columbia and started negotiating agreements on land and self-government with the Aboriginal peoples.

The Movement Toward National Political Organizations

Following World War I, there were further attempts at political organization, this time in Ontario. Thousands of Aboriginal people had made a significant contribution to the war effort and they believed they had a right to make their voices heard. In 1919 Frederick O. Loft, himself a war veteran, formed the League of Indians of Canada. The League was the first attempt to create a national

Figure 20-1 The Nisga'a of Nass River in British Columbia made an official land claim to Ottawa in 1913. The issue was a spark for Aboriginal political activism throughout the century. On August 4, 1998 a treaty between the Nisga'a people and the B.C. and federal governments was finally negotiated. It gives the Nisga'a 1922 square kilometres of land in the lower Nass Valley, self-government powers much like municipal governments, $190 million in cash, and resource rights over their lands which allows access to the fishery and forests. The Nisga'a can set up their own courts but the Criminal Code and Constitution of Canada apply. The treaty has been ratified by the Nisga'a but must still be ratified by the provincial and federal governments. In this photo, a Nisga'a drummer celebrates the landmark treaty.

voice for Aboriginal peoples. Loft pressed for greater control over band funds and property and was determined that Aboriginal peoples should have the right to vote in federal and provincial elections without giving up their Indian status. The federal government tried to undermine Loft by removing his Indian status and by refusing Aboriginal people the right to use band funds to attend League meetings.

In the 1920s, Reverend Edward Ahenakew, a Cree, helped extend the League into Western Canada. Throughout the 1920s and 1930s, the League argued for improved health and education programs, increased economic aid, control over reserve lands, and the right to hunt, fish, and trap without government interference. Protests were also made against bans on traditional ceremonies such as the sun dance, the pass system, and the purchase of reserve lands by the federal government.

The League eventually lost momentum because it was difficult to gain nationwide support. The diversity of Aboriginal peoples has made unity difficult. Status and Non-Status Indians and treaty and non-treaty Indians often have different political agendas and opinions about how to solve the complex problems facing their communities.

In 1961, another attempt was made with the National Indian Council which eventually split into the National Indian Brotherhood (representing status and treaty groups) and the Native Council of Canada (representing Non-Status Indians and Métis). These organizations came to play a major role in the opposition to the proposals of the Trudeau government in the late 1960s and 1970s, and the constitutional conferences in the 1980s. Since the early 1960s, Aboriginal peoples have had strong national organizations representing their views in the political arena.

Figure 20-2 Frederick Ogilvie Loft was active in forming the League of Indians of Canada in 1919.

CONNECTIONS

SOME POLITICAL ORGANIZATIONS REPRESENTING ABORIGINAL PEOPLES TODAY

Assembly of First Nations (AFN)
Established in 1982 from a reorganization of the National Indian Brotherhood. Represents status and treaty First Nations peoples in Canada. Aims to develop common strategies on issues such as Aboriginal and treaty rights, economic development, housing, education, health, social services, land claims, and self-government.

Inuit Tapirisat of Canada (ITC)
Formed in 1971 to promote Inuit culture and identity and to present a common front on political, economic and environmental issues concerning the Inuit. Represents the more than 41 000 Inuit living in the Northwest Territories, Nunavut, Nunavik, Labrador and other areas of Canada. Played a major role in the negotiations for the new territory of Nunavut.

Congress of Aboriginal Peoples
Established in 1994 as a coalition of urban and off-reserve Indians, Non-Status Indians, Indians who gained their status under Bill C-31 in 1985 but did not gain band membership, and Métis outside the Prairies. This organization evolved from the Native Council of Canada (NCC) which was established in 1970 to represent Métis and Non-Status Indians.

Métis National Council
Formed in 1983 when it broke away from the Native Council of Canada. Represents the Métis of Manitoba, Alberta and Saskatchewan who see themselves as distinct from Non-Status Indians and Métis in other parts of the country. They are the descendants of the historic Métis of western Canada with political concerns of their own, many related to historic injustices. Seek rights to a land base and self-government for its people.

RECONNECT

1. Choose two of the organizations discussed in the reading and explain why each was formed.

2. What challenges did Aboriginal organizations face?

FOCUS

This section will help you understand
  a. the changing federal response to Aboriginal issues in the North in the 1970s
  b. the importance of the James Bay and Northern Quebec Agreement and the Mackenzie Valley Pipeline Inquiry
  c. new land settlements affecting the North.

Making Inroads

During the development boom in the 1950s and 1960s, the interests of Aboriginal peoples were often ignored. In the 1970s, with the development of more effective political organizations, Aboriginal peoples began to make their voices heard. Key events occurred in the North. The James Bay Agreement in 1975 and the Mackenzie Valley Pipeline Inquiry in 1978 were turning points in the relationship between Aboriginal peoples and governments.

The James Bay and Northern Quebec Agreement of 1975

In 1971, the Quebec government led by Robert Bourassa and Hydro-Québec designed a massive hydroelectric project which would flood 10 000 square kilometres east of James Bay. The project was meant to create close to 100 000 jobs and reap the benefits of the electric power potential in the

Figure 21-1 Thomas Berger travelled to communities throughout the Mackenzie Valley region to listen to the views of Aboriginal people on the pipeline proposal. This photo was taken at Nahanni Butte, Northwest Territories.

province's northern rivers. But the government and Hydro-Québec did not consider the rights and interests of the nearly 10 000 Cree and Inuit who lived in the area. Together the Cree, led by Chief Billy Diamond of the Waskaganish band, and the Inuit, led by the Inuit Tapirisat, took legal action to stop the project until their rights were established. No treaties had ever been signed in the region and the peoples believed they had Aboriginal title to the lands.

The Cree and Inuit succeeded in having the work stopped. Though work started again after a court appeal, the issue of Aboriginal claim to the land was not resolved. The government decided to negotiate with the Cree and Inuit rather than risk a lengthy court battle that could seriously affect work on the project. Late in 1975, an agreement was signed.

Under the James Bay and Northern Quebec Agreement, the Cree and Inuit received $232.5 million over 20 years, special economic assistance, outright ownership of 5500 square kilometres of land, hunting and fishing rights over 129 500 square kilometres of undeveloped land, and a **veto** over mineral resource development. In the years since the agreement, however, optimism has lessened. There have been severe negative effects on the environment and the lives of the Aboriginal people.

The Mackenzie Valley Pipeline Inquiry of 1974-1977

Pressure to develop energy resources also occurred in the Arctic in the 1970s. In 1974, a royal commission led by Justice Thomas Berger was set up to investigate construction of an oil and gas pipeline along the Mackenzie Valley. The pipeline was to be the largest construction project ever in the North.

In 1977, the Berger Commission Report recommended that construction be delayed for at least 10 years because of potential damage to the environ-ment and traditional Aboriginal lifestyles. Berger pointed to the effects a sudden influx of outsiders would have on Aboriginal peoples and recom-mended that land claims be settled first. In the end, the pipeline was never built.

EyeWitness

Voices from the Mackenzie Valley Pipeline Inquiry

To really bring the whole picture into focus, you can describe it as the rape of the northland to satisfy the greed and the needs of southern consumers, and when development of this nature happens, it only destroys; it does not leave any permanent jobs for people who make the North their home. The whole process does not leave very much for us to be proud of, and along with their equipment and technology, they also impose on the northern people their white culture and all its value systems.

—Louise Frost, Old Crow, Yukon Territory quoted in *Northern Frontier, Northern Homeland*.

We look upon the North as our last frontier. It is natural for us to think of developing it, of subduing the land and extracting its resources to fuel Canada's industry and heat our homes. Our whole inclination is to think of expanding our industrial machine to the limit of our country's frontiers.... But the native people say that the North is their homeland. They have lived there for thousands of years. They claim it is their land, and they believe they have a right to say what its future ought to be.

—Thomas Berger quoted in *Northern Frontier, Northern Homeland*.

Figure 21-2 Until the 1970s, only two treaties covered land north of the sixtieth parallel. Since the 1970s, Canadian gov-ernments and Aboriginal peoples in the North have signed several important land agreements. These new agreements require Aboriginal people to give up title to large areas of land in return for both lump sum and annual cash payments, and hunting and fishing rights. But unlike previous treaties, these agreements also give Aboriginal people outright own-ership of land and some degree of self-government.

Other Developments in the North

The James Bay Agreement and Berger Commission Report set the stage for further land claim and self-government agreements in the North. In 1984 the governments of Canada and Quebec passed the Cree-Naskapi Act. The Act replaces the Indian Act and allows band councils to pass laws affecting land and resource use, band funds, and cultural devel-opment. In cases of conflict with provincial laws, legislation passed by the band council prevails. Many people consider this Act the first example of Aboriginal self-government in Canada.

Starting in the late 1980s, the federal government negotiated agreements with the Inuvialuit of the western Arctic, several First Nations in the Yukon, the Gwich'in of the Mackenzie River valley, and the Sahtu Dene and Métis of the Great Bear Lake region in the Northwest Territories. These agree-ments involve varying degrees of Aboriginal self-gov-ernment including the use of traditional Aboriginal knowledge when making decisions about land use. In 1992, the agreement for Nunavut was signed.

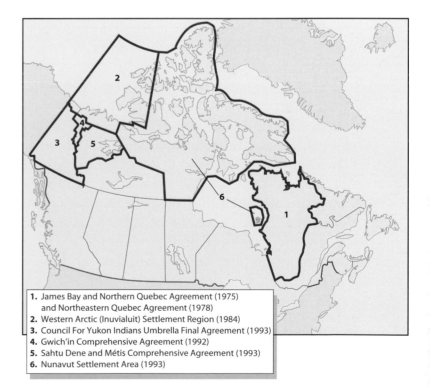

1. James Bay and Northern Quebec Agreement (1975) and Northeastern Quebec Agreement (1978)
2. Western Arctic (Inuvialuit) Settlement Region (1984)
3. Council For Yukon Indians Umbrella Final Agreement (1993)
4. Gwich'in Comprehensive Agreement (1992)
5. Sahtu Dene and Métis Comprehensive Agreement (1993)
6. Nunavut Settlement Area (1993)

RECONNECT

1. Note three features of recent government-Aboriginal agreements in the North.

2. What appear to be the major Aboriginal concerns with respect to Northern development?

FOCUS

This section will help you understand
    a. the changing relationship between governments and Aboriginal people since the 1960s
    b. Aboriginal responses to government actions since the 1980s.

The White Paper, 1969

Through the 1970s and 1980s as Aboriginal people continued to gain a stronger political voice, they began to have some effective influence over government decisions. The process, however, was full of roadblocks and frustrations.

The White Paper on Aboriginal policy, issued by the Liberal government of Pierre Trudeau in 1969, was a turning point. Trudeau had campaigned on a platform of belief in a "just society" and a democracy in which all citizens could participate equally. The government also committed to changing the policy toward Aboriginal peoples and to consulting them about the changes. Aboriginal leaders were optimistic, but when all was said and done the government's new policy brought a storm of protest from Aboriginal peoples.

The government stated that the major aim of the White Paper was to enable Aboriginal peoples to be "free to develop Indian cultures in an environment of legal, social, and economic equality with other Canadians." The belief was that the special status of Aboriginal peoples had set them apart from other Canadians and prevented their development. The White Paper, therefore, proposed to do away with the Indian Act, give Indians control of their reserves, dismantle the Department of Indian

Affairs, shift all responsibility for Aboriginal peoples to the provinces and eventually eliminate treaty rights. To most Aboriginal peoples, however, this was another call for their assimilation and a denial of their basic rights.

The National Indian Brotherhood (later the Assembly of First Nations) took a decisive stand against the proposals. Another key figure in the forefront of opposition was Harold Cardinal, then the young leader of the Indian Association of Alberta. Cardinal was a fiery speaker who forcefully denounced the government's policies. He also took a leading role in presenting a response to the government known as the Red Paper. The government eventually withdrew the White Paper in 1970. Aboriginal peoples had reasserted their Aboriginal and treaty rights.

Figure 22-1 Relations between Aboriginal peoples and the federal government in the decade after the White Paper were often tense and stormy. One of the most notable incidents occurred in 1974 when a group of Aboriginal people from Vancouver and an RCMP riot squad clashed on Parliament Hill in Ottawa. The Aboriginal people were part of the "Native Peoples' Caravan," which was meant to be a peaceful protest against poor living conditions. The riot squad, and then the military, was called in to deal with the protest. This was the first time such measures had been taken against Aboriginal demonstrators.

CROSSFIRE

THE WHITE PAPER AND
ABORIGINAL OPPOSITION

[I]n our policy…we won't recognize Aboriginal rights. We will recognize treaty rights. We will recognize forms of contract which have been made with the Indian people by the Crown and we will try to bring justice in that area and this will mean that perhaps the treaties shouldn't go on forever. It's inconceivable, I think, that in a given society one section of the society have a treaty with the other section of the society. We must be all equal under the laws, and we must not sign treaties amongst ourselves.

—Pierre Trudeau, Prime Minister of Canada quoted in *The Indian: Assimilation, Integration, or Separation?*

The new Indian policy…is a thinly disguised programme of extermination through assimilation. For the Indian to survive, says the government in effect, he must become a good little brown white man. Americans to the south of us used to have a saying: "The only good Indian is a dead Indian." The [new programme] would amend this but slightly to, "The only good Indian is a non-Indian."
    The federal government, instead of acknowledging its legal and moral responsibilities to the Indians of Canada and honouring the treaties that the Indians signed in good faith, now proposes to wash its hands of Indians entirely…

—Harold Cardinal, *The Unjust Society: The Tragedy of Canada's Indians.*

Figure 22-2 Harold Cardinal's book *The Unjust Society* was a scathing attack on the government's policy toward Aboriginal peoples.

The Charter of Rights and Freedoms, 1982

In 1980, Prime Minister Trudeau proposed changing the Constitution of Canada and adding a Charter of Rights and Freedoms. Aboriginal leaders wanted to be included in the constitutional talks. As "nations" within Canada, they believed they had the right to participate equally with the provincial premiers at first ministers conferences. They were not given the opportunity to participate and when the Charter was drafted, it did not include terms to protect the rights of either women or Aboriginal peoples. Aboriginal leaders campaigned nationally and internationally to get protection for their rights into the new Charter. Finally, their efforts were successful. In 1982, the new Charter officially recognized Indians, Métis, and Inuit as Aboriginal peoples with special Aboriginal and treaty rights.

The exact definition of "Aboriginal rights," however, was still an issue. Aboriginal leaders believed that they included not only rights to original lands and the right to practise their beliefs and culture, but an automatic or **inherent right** to self-government. Canadian governments disagreed: Aboriginal self-government would be a gift given to Aboriginal peoples by the government, not an inherent right. While discussions in the 1980s could not solve this problem, Aboriginal leaders continued to push for self-government.

Primary Source
THE CANADIAN CHARTER OF RIGHTS AND FREEDOMS

A summary of the major provisions relating to Aboriginal peoples:

◆ The Aboriginal peoples are defined as including the Indian, Inuit and Métis peoples.

◆ The existing Aboriginal and treaty rights of the Aboriginal peoples of Canada are "recognized and affirmed".

◆ The Charter's guarantee of other rights and freedoms may not take away from or negate "any Aboriginal, treaty or other rights or freedoms that pertain to the Aboriginal peoples of Canada" including rights or freedoms recognized by the Royal Proclamation of 1763, and any rights or freedoms acquired by way of land claims settlement.

◆ An amendment that came into effect in 1984 also enshrined Aboriginal people's rights and freedoms obtained through land claims agreements past or future, and guaranteed all the rights equally to men and women. The amendment also stated that there could be no changes to the Constitution relating to "Indians and Indian reserves" or Aboriginal rights and freedoms guaranteed in the Charter without discussions at a conference of First Ministers with representatives of Aboriginal peoples.

—Eugene Forsey *How Canadians Govern Themselves*.

From Meech Lake to Charlottetown

The province of Quebec had not signed the new Constitution in 1982, so in 1987 Conservative Prime Minister Brian Mulroney and the provincial governments devised the Meech Lake Accord. The Accord offered to recognize Quebec as a "distinct society" with special status, but did not mention self-government for Aboriginal peoples.

Once again Aboriginal leaders were outraged. They believed they had at least as much right to distinct society status as Quebec. Prime Minister Mulroney had allowed three years for all provincial legislatures to formally agree to the Accord. As the deadline approached, Newfoundland, New Brunswick, and Manitoba still opposed the deal. As pressure to agree mounted, the premier of Manitoba decided to hold a final vote in the provincial legislature. The vote had to be unanimous for the Accord to pass. In a dramatic moment, Elijah Harper, the only Aboriginal member of the Manitoba Legislature, voiced his vote: "No." His action effectively ended the Accord. Harper later said; "We blocked the Accord because it posed a threat to Aboriginal people. Aboriginal people have no quarrel with Quebec. But we're a distinct society too, and we've fought for many years for the basic rights that Quebec takes for granted, such as participating in constitutional talks."

In 1992, Prime Minister Mulroney again tried to get Quebec to sign a constitutional deal. This time the new agreement, known as the Charlottetown Accord, guaranteed Aboriginal self-government. Not all Aboriginal leaders supported the agreement but it soon made little difference. The Accord was defeated in a national **referendum**. There have been no constitutional discussions since that time although some recent land claims agreements give a degree of self-government to Aboriginal people.

Figure 22-3 Aboriginal peoples were shut out of the constitutional talks. Above, protestors opposed to the Meech Lake Accord, demonstrate outside the Manitoba Legislature.

BIOGRAPHY

Subject: Elijah Harper

Dates: Born in 1949

Figure 22-4   Elijah Harper.

Most Notable Accomplishment: Made the decisive move that defeated the Meech Lake Accord in the Manitoba legislature in 1992 because it did not recognize Aboriginal rights; has worked throughout his career for recognition of Aboriginal peoples' concerns in Canada and abroad.

Thumbnail Sketch: Elijah Harper, a Cree, was born at Red Sucker Lake in northeastern Manitoba. Until the age of six, Harper was raised in the traditional way by his grandparents and he gained a sense of the land, animals, and his people. His father then sent him to a residential school to get an education. Despite the experiences of humiliation and strict regulation, he developed a sense of inner strength.

As a teen, he joined the Manitoba Association of Native Youth at a time when the civil rights movement was emerging in North America. He also became involved in the Aboriginal political movement in Manitoba. In 1971, he entered the University of Manitoba where his political awareness had a chance to develop further. His career path took him through work with the Manitoba Department of Education and the Department of Northern Affairs on Aboriginal projects and an election as chief at Red Sucker Lake. In 1981, he ran for the NDP in the Manitoba provincial election and won. He became the first Aboriginal MLA in Manitoba's history and represented a constituency whose population was mainly Aboriginal.

From then on, his involvement in national Aboriginal affairs increased. He became a dedicated supporter of Aboriginal self-government and land claims, working with other Aboriginal leaders in Canada and abroad. In 1992, he stood by these convictions when he rejected the Meech Lake Accord in the Manitoba Legislature. Since that dramatic moment, he has continued to work for Aboriginal concerns, both in the political arena nationally and internationally and as a spiritual leader. After a serious illness in 1992, he had a vision that he could work toward Aboriginal unity and healing. He organized an international gathering of spiritual leaders in 1995. He was involved in the historic agreement in which Manitoba bands received powers of self-government in 1994 and he was part of a delegation that travelled to South Africa in 1996 to help in their transition from **apartheid** to self-government. He saw many parallels between the experiences of Aboriginal peoples in Canada and Black people in South Africa. Increasingly he is becoming actively involved in issues affecting Aboriginal peoples around the world and he has spoken at the United Nations and other international organizations.

Significant Quote: "I have always stressed that our people should be involved in the political process… It is important to be involved in not only Indian politics, but mainstream politics, because no one is going to speak for us. If you rely on someone for your freedom, you will never be a free man.

"After enduring so many years of injustice, Aboriginal people are working to redress the inequities imposed upon our nations and communities. My role in Meech Lake was one small contribution to the struggle of Aboriginal people for recognition and rights. I was proud to be able to advance the cause from within the political structure. There was born a new pride and a knowledge that we can make a difference, that we can direct the future of our country."

RECONNECT

1. Harold Cardinal said the White Paper implied "The only good Indian is a non-Indian." List three proposals of the White Paper which could justify his comment.

2. How did the Charter of Rights and Freedoms advance the cause of Aboriginal peoples?

Land Claims

FOCUS

This section will help you understand
   a. Aboriginal and legal viewpoints regarding land claims
   b. the challenges involved in filing and settling land claims.

> **All of our structures and values have developed out of a spiritual relationship with the land on which we have lived.**
> —George Manuel, Shuswap Grand Chief and past President of the World Council of Indigenous Peoples.

A New Era in the Courts

In 1973, the Supreme Court of Canada ruled that Aboriginal people who had not signed treaties still had some claim to their traditional lands. This was the first judgment involving Aboriginal land rights since the signing of the numbered treaties between 1871 and 1929. As a result of this decision, the federal government established an office to deal with Aboriginal land claims.

TIMELINE ⟶ Contemporary Milestones

1990 — The Government of Canada establishes a Royal Commission on Aboriginal Peoples (RCAP).

1992 — The Nunavut land claim agreement is signed.

1993 — The National Aboriginal Achievement Awards are established in Canada.

1993 — The UN Working Group on Indigenous Populations completes a Draft Declaration on the Rights of Indigenous Peoples.

1993 — The UN General Assembly proclaims the International Year of the World's Indigenous People.

1995 — The UN General Assembly proclaims the period 1995 to 2004 as the International Decade of the World's Indigenous People, calling on governments to address the problems of Indigenous populations.

1996 — June 21 is officially declared National Aboriginal Day in Canada.

1996 — The Aboriginal owned-and-operated First Nations Bank of Canada is officially launched.

1996 — The RCAP releases its report, recommending a renewed relationship between Aboriginal and non-Aboriginal people based on justice and fairness.

1998 — Minister of Indian Affairs and Northern Development Jane Stewart makes a Statement of Reconciliation on behalf of the Government of Canada, apologizing to victims of sexual and physical abuse at residential schools and allocating $350 million to support the development of community-based healing.

1998 — *An Agenda for Action with First Nations*, announced jointly by the federal government and the Assembly of First Nations, outlines how the Government of Canada and First Nations can work as partners.

1998 — The first modern treaty is negotiated by the Nisga'a Nation, British Columbia, and Canada, and is expected to be a model for future Aboriginal self-government agreements.

1999 — New territory of Nunavut is officially established.

Types of Land Claims

Aboriginal groups can file one of two types of land claims, depending on whether or not they signed treaties with Canadian governments in the past. In areas where treaties exist, Aboriginal people may make **specific claims** on the basis that federal or provincial governments violated treaty rights. Some specific claims have been rejected while others are still being negotiated.

Comprehensive claims can be made in areas where First Nations and Canadian governments did not sign treaties. Such claims, already bolstered by the 1973 Supreme Court judgment, were further strengthened by a 1997 Supreme Court ruling. The 1997 decision stated that traditional lands are "owned" by the entire Aboriginal community using and occupying them. The court also reaffirmed the value of oral evidence in determining traditional patterns of land ownership. This was a very significant ruling—before it was made, unoccupied traditional lands were controlled by the government, and Aboriginal people maintained only certain hunting and trapping rights on the land.

Time will tell how the 1997 ruling will affect future land claims. Up until the ruling, the work involved in settling comprehensive land claims was time-consuming and difficult, and may continue to be so. The first step is proving that an Aboriginal group, as an organized society, has occupied the land "since time immemorial." Problems arise in cases like the Ojibwa First Nation, who changed territories in some places after the arrival of Europeans in North America. The research needed to prove a group's historical right can take from two to five years.

If for any reason the federal government does not agree that a land claim is valid, the claims process ends without the possibility of appeal except through the courts. Even if the process reaches the negotiation stage, the federal government controls the pace of negotiation. In successful land claims, the parties usually agree to transfers of specified amounts of cash and land from governments to Aboriginal communities.

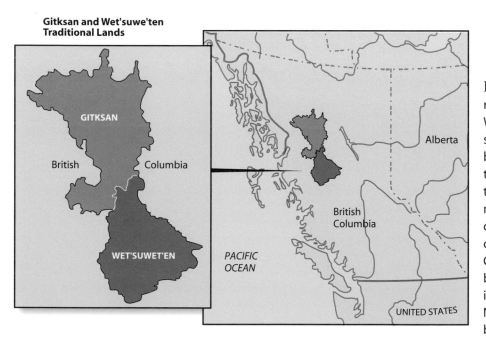

Figure 23-1 The 1997 Supreme Court ruling established that the Gitksan and Wet'suwet'en bands of British Columbia still owned their traditional lands. The bands have been trying to protect this traditional area of 58 000 square kilometres (about the size of Nova Scotia) from non-Aboriginal people since 1866. Their court battle began in 1984. Many other comprehensive claims in British Columbia and eastern Canada remain to be settled. Comprehensive claims covering much of northern Canada, including Nunavut and the James Bay area, have been finalized.

RECONNECT

1. Describe two types of land claims.

2. Do you personally agree or disagree with the current land claims procedures in Canada? Explain fully.

The Inherent Right to Self-government

Before Europeans settled in Canada in the 17th century, Aboriginal people governed themselves in organized societies. For example, the Haudenosaunee (Iroquois Confederacy) were structured into households, clans, and nations. Each nation had its own territories and councils of *sachems* (chiefs), and relations among the nations of the Confederacy were governed by an oral constitution. In some areas in British Columbia, each First Nation orally recounted laws, traditions, and clan histories in order to maintain peace. As with any human institutions, those of Aboriginal societies had evolved and changed over time, and would have continued to do so given the opportunity.

In the early years of contact, Europeans recognized that Aboriginal societies truly were independent nations. That recognition almost disappeared during the next two centuries, and resurfaced only in the 1970s. By that time, Aboriginal activists had forced the federal government to consider the idea of Aboriginal self-government. But the government viewed self-government as a gift to be bestowed by Canada on Aboriginal peoples. Aboriginal peoples rejected that viewpoint, asserting that they had an inherent right to govern themselves. An inherent right is a right that automatically belongs to people, rather than a gift that people receive. Aboriginal peoples argued that their right to self-government existed because their societies historically had been organized and self-ruling. Today, Aboriginal leaders insist that the Canadian Constitution should be changed to include the inherent right of Aboriginal peoples to govern themselves.

Primary Source

A STATEMENT ON ABORIGINAL SELF-GOVERNMENT

We all believe...that as First Nations we should have our own governments with jurisdiction over our own lands and people.

We should decide about and benefit from the type of development we want in our own territories, not have such development forced on us to serve outside interests.

We should have tribal courts run by our own people. We should administer our own child-care and social services. We should take control over our own education....

In effect, then, we would be participants in a bilateral agreement with the federal government. Provinces would no longer have authority over us in our own lands, and whenever federal-provincial agreements were negotiated, we would be included, accorded a role similar to that of provinces today....[W]e would be regarded as a third participant, a separate founding nation, exercising control over its own territories.

—Georges Erasmus, past Grand Chief of the Assembly of First Nations and Co-chair of the Royal Commission on Aboriginal Peoples quoted in Boyce Richardson, ed., *Drumbeat: Anger and Renewal in Indian Country* (Toronto: Summerhill, 1989), pp. 2-3.

Figure 24-1 Federal and provincial governments and Aboriginal leaders agreed in 1992 that the inherent right to Aboriginal self-government must be explicitly affirmed in the Canadian Constitution. This and other changes to the Constitution were specified in the Charlottetown Accord. Above, Ovide Mercredi sells the Accord to Quebec chiefs. Canadians, however, rejected the Accord in a nationwide referendum.

TIMELINE Achievements in Self-government

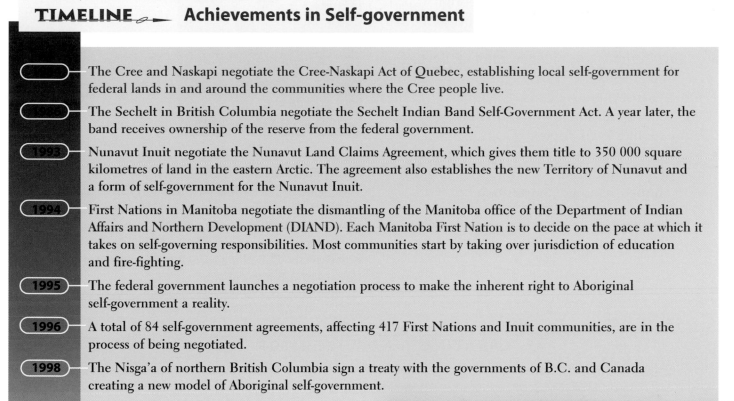

The Cree and Naskapi negotiate the Cree-Naskapi Act of Quebec, establishing local self-government for federal lands in and around the communities where the Cree people live.

1986 — The Sechelt in British Columbia negotiate the Sechelt Indian Band Self-Government Act. A year later, the band receives ownership of the reserve from the federal government.

1993 — Nunavut Inuit negotiate the Nunavut Land Claims Agreement, which gives them title to 350 000 square kilometres of land in the eastern Arctic. The agreement also establishes the new Territory of Nunavut and a form of self-government for the Nunavut Inuit.

1994 — First Nations in Manitoba negotiate the dismantling of the Manitoba office of the Department of Indian Affairs and Northern Development (DIAND). Each Manitoba First Nation is to decide on the pace at which it takes on self-governing responsibilities. Most communities start by taking over jurisdiction of education and fire-fighting.

1995 — The federal government launches a negotiation process to make the inherent right to Aboriginal self-government a reality.

1996 — A total of 84 self-government agreements, affecting 417 First Nations and Inuit communities, are in the process of being negotiated.

1998 — The Nisga'a of northern British Columbia sign a treaty with the governments of B.C. and Canada creating a new model of Aboriginal self-government.

Making Self-government a Reality

Self-government means that Aboriginal peoples will control such matters as social services, health care, education, resource development, culture, language and justice. As well, First Nations bands will decide who can join the band and how band government will be organized. In some cases, these aspects of self-government have already been achieved. Many First Nations in the North gained control over resource development in the 1980s and 1990s through comprehensive land claims agreements. Bands have had the option of controlling band membership since 1985. About one-quarter of Canadian bands had taken such control as of 1995.

The 1996 Report of the Royal Commission on Aboriginal Peoples (RCAP) makes several recommendations, some controversial, about the form Aboriginal self-government should take. These include:

▶ applying self-government to Aboriginal *nations* (First Nations, Inuit, and Métis) rather than to small *communities*. (There are an estimated 60 to 80 historical Aboriginal nations in Canada, while the number of Aboriginal communities is

Figure 24-2 Phil Fontaine and Indian Affairs Minister Ron Irwin sign the Manitoba Dismantling Framework Agreement in 1994. The experience of Manitoba First Nations will be a model for dismantling the Department of Indian Affairs and Northern Development across the country.

about 1000.) These Aboriginal governments may vary in structure, reflecting the different traditions of separate nations.

▶ establishing a House of First Peoples as an Aboriginal parliament, representing Aboriginal governments as an order equal to the federal and provincial governments.

▶ establishing dual citizenship for Aboriginal people as citizens of Canada and of an Aboriginal nation.

▶ getting funding for self-government by taxing Aboriginal citizens rather than by transferring money from land claims payments. (Other Canadian governments should continue to pay some monies to Aboriginal governments).

▶ establishing the laws of Aboriginal nations by way of referendums in which Aboriginal citizens vote on their nation's Constitution.

Figure 24-3 Andrew Bear Robe is the Program Director for Aboriginal Leadership and Self-Government programs at The Banff Centre for Management in Alberta. These programs train Aboriginal leaders to put into practice the inherent right to Aboriginal self-government, now recognized by the Canadian government. Mr. Bear Robe is now currently president and CEO of the Nicola Valley Institute of Technology at Merrit, British Columbia.

CaseStudy

CREATING A NEW TERRITORY

The RCAP Report outlined three models for Aboriginal self-government. One is *nation* government operating on a land base, which could apply throughout the country wherever land claims have been settled. The second is a *community-of-interest* government, which would apply to Aboriginal people in urban centres without a land base. The third is *public* government, which is the model to be followed by the new territory of Nunavut.

Nunavut means "Our Land" in the Inuit language of Inuktitut. Inuit have lived continuously in the central and eastern Arctic for thousands of years. Today, they make up about 85% of the region's population.

The Inuit of Nunavut have been working towards a land claims settlement and self-government since 1974, after changes to their way of life had become increasingly disruptive. One distressing change was the invasion of the land by resource industries exploring for oil and minerals. Organizations such as the Inuit Tapirisat of Canada and the Tungavik Federation of Nunavut devoted themselves to protecting the region from such exploitation and giving Inuit a political voice. On May 25, 1993, two decades of hard work were rewarded. The Nunavut Land Claims Agreement made Nunavut Inuit the largest private land owners in North America.

A provision of the agreement was the separation of the eastern half of the Northwest Territories to create the new territory of Nunavut on April 1, 1999. Within this publicly governed territory of 1 235 200 square kilometres, the Nunavut Inuit own and control the resources of 355 842 square kilometres of land. Other benefits to the Inuit provided by the agreement include:

• equal representation with government on boards managing the territory's wildlife, resources, and environment
• transfer payments of $1.148 billion payable over 14 years
• a $13 million trust fund for training in leadership, management, and public service
• a share of federal government royalties from oil, gas, and mineral development on Crown lands.

The Nunavut Implementation Commission (NIC) was established to plan for the territorial government of Nunavut. It will be a public government representing all residents of Nunavut by way of a democratically elected Legislative Assembly.

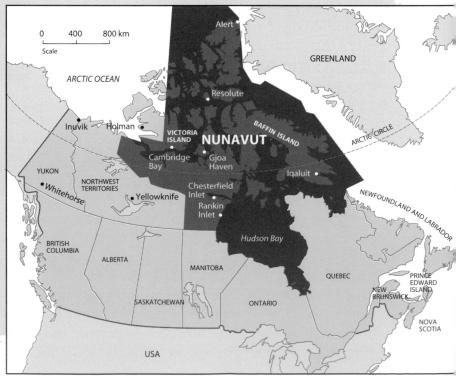

Figure 24-4 On April 1, 1999, the territory of Nunavut comes into being. Its area is one-fifth the total area of Canada, and its population is 85% Inuit.

BIOGRAPHY

Subject: Rosemarie Kuptana

Dates: Born in 1954

Most Notable Accomplishment: Kuptana "was instrumental in securing recognition of the inherent right of Aboriginal people to self-government."

Thumbnail Sketch: After growing up in a traditional Inuit hunting society, Kuptana spent ten painful years at a residential school. There, she lost her ability to speak in her mother tongue of Inuvialuktun. In 1979 she began work as a broadcaster with the CBC and eventually became president of the Inuit Broadcasting Corporation (IBC). As a leader in broadcasting, she helped develop programs in Inuktitut about Inuit traditions and politics. From 1986 to 1989, she was Canadian vice-president of the Inuit Circumpolar Conference, an international organization. From 1991 to 1996 she served as president of the political organization the Inuit Tapirisat of Canada. During this eventful period, she participated in planning for Nunavut and was the lead negotiator in the Charlottetown Accord talks. These talks resulted in government recognition of the inherent right to Aboriginal self-government. In 1995, Kuptana became president of the Inuit Circumpolar Conference, where she focuses on resource management and environmental issues as well as political concerns.

Figure 24-5 Rosemarie Kuptana.

Significant Quote: "Inuit have waited a long time for this moment [the constitutional talks]. Within our grasp as Canadian Inuit is the recognition that we are equal to others with inherent rights and powers to ensure our continued existence within Canada…Our hopes have never been higher."

Concerns About Self-government

Concerns about self-government include: the power of chiefs and councils; the rights of women; the situation of Aboriginal people not living on Aboriginal-owned land; the situation of non-Aboriginal people living on land that becomes part of an Aboriginal nation through land claims settlements.

In many communities that are moving toward self-government, the chief and council have total control of finances and administration. The challenge for communities will be to create a government with checks and balances to guard against misuse of administrative powers.

Some Aboriginal women worry that, as citizens of Aboriginal nations, they will not be protected by the Charter of Rights and Freedoms. The challenge will be to create systems that give women a voice and protect them against abuse and discrimination.

Finally, who will have jurisdiction over and responsibility for Aboriginal peoples who do not live on reserves? In a related issue, what will happen to non-Aboriginal people living on land that becomes part of an Aboriginal nation through a land claims settlement?

Creating systems of government is one of the most challenging tasks humans face. For Aboriginal nations, consultation and the determination to change the systems that have failed them will be important steps in achieving self-government throughout Canada.

RECONNECT

1. In your own words, explain the term "inherent right to self-government."

2. Outline your reactions to the proposal to create a House of First Peoples.

3. Identify two important features of the new government of Nunavut.

FOCUS

This section will help you understand
a. the reasons for protest among Aboriginal peoples
b. ways in which they have carried out their protests.

> "For healing to begin...[w]e must acknowledge the wrong that has been done...Facts and feelings must be faced, squarely, before we can move beyond them. Denying pain and anger does not make these emotions go away.
>
> —Erica-Irene Daes, Chairperson, UN Working Group on Indigenous Populations.

The Struggle For Recognition

For over two centuries, Canada has been officially described as a country founded by two nations or peoples—the French and the English. Such an understanding gives no consideration to the presence and role of Aboriginal groups throughout history. It has resulted in the denial of Aboriginal rights. While the federal government now acknowledges these rights, it has taken years. Some Aboriginal people, frustrated with the slow pace of recognition, have used protests to bring their concerns to the Canadian public.

Protecting Land and Environment

In several cases, Aboriginal groups have objected to uses of the environment by non-Aboriginal groups. A long-standing example is the protest of the Innu Nation against low-level flying in Labrador.

In 1964, the Canadian military began allowing NATO (North Atlantic Treaty Organization) forces to fly aircraft in

Figure 25-1 An Innu woman supports Innu arrested on charges of public mischief while protesting against low-level military training flights. Innu women have played an important role in the fight against low-level flying.

Low-Level Training Areas (LLTAs) in Labrador. These training flights—only 30 metres aboveground and at speeds over 1000 kilometres an hour—disturb the habitats of birds, caribou, moose, and other noise-sensitive species. The training routes overlap with Innu hunting territory and thus threaten the livelihood of Innu and other hunters. The Innu first expressed concern about the environmental impact of the flights in 1980, writing letters to the federal environment minister. When their concerns were ignored, they launched a campaign to stop the flights. They wrote letters to the Department of National Defence, organized joint actions with rural peoples and Aboriginal groups in the U.S. and Europe, met with European government representatives, held news conferences, and participated in demonstrations. Still failing to stop the flights, the Innu began a campaign of civil disobedience in 1987. They camped out on bomber testing ranges and blocked runways with their bodies. Many people were arrested and jailed during the campaign. Although these efforts resulted in the cancellation of a proposed $500 million expansion at the Goose Bay military base in Labrador, the low-level training flights continue.

The Oka crisis in 1990 may be one of the most widely-publicized Aboriginal protests of recent times. On March 11, a group of Mohawks from Kanesatake, west of Montreal, erected roadblocks to stop the construction of a golf course on disputed land at Oka, Quebec. When Mohawks ignored court orders to clear the road, about 100 Quebec

Provincial Police tried to dismantle the roadblocks by force. Gunfire resulted and one officer died. Canadian soldiers, called in by the Quebec government, settled into a stand-off with Mohawk protesters that lasted 11 weeks and resulted in the arrests of the protesters. These events capped a complicated 300-year struggle over the land at Oka.

Figure 25-2
Mohawk protesters raise the flag over their barricade in Oka during the 11-week crisis in 1990.

In 1993, members of the Kettle and Stoney Point Band near Sarnia, Ontario reoccupied part of the nearby provincial campground at Ipperwash. This land had been taken from the band during World War II for use as a military base. Eighteen families were removed from the land with the promise that they would be able to return after the war. The military base remained, however, and every request by the Kettle and Stoney Point Band for the return of the land was rejected by the government. A second occupation of the disputed area took place in 1995, during which a police officer killed an unarmed protester. In 1998, after 56 years, an agreement-in-principle was signed returning the land to the band. The agreement also gives the band $26 million for damages, healing, and economic development.

Figure 25-3 In 1995, two Aboriginal protesters protect a barricade near the entrance to Ipperwash Provincial Park.

TIMELINE ⌀— The Struggle Over Oka

1717	The government of France gives a land grant at Oka to the Roman Catholic Order of St.-Sulpice. It is used as a refuge for nearly 700 Six Nations Iroquois and Huron, as well as Algonkian and Nipissing people.
1788	The First Nations occupying Oka claim title to the land. The British government rejects the claim.
1822	The Algonkian and Nipissing occupying Oka claim title to the lands on both sides of the Ottawa River. The British government rejects the claim in 1827.
1869	The Canadian government moves some First Nations people from Oka to a location further up the Ottawa River.
1933	Sulpicians sell off 100 lots at Oka to repay a debt owed to the Province of Quebec.
1945	The federal government purchases the remaining Sulpician lands at Oka.
1959	The municipality of Oka builds a nine-hole golf course at Oka.
1961	A group of First Nations requests that the Oka lands be given reserve status. The federal government denies the request.
1975	The Office of Native Claims rejects a comprehensive land claim made by the Mohawks covering the Oka lands.
1986	The Office of Native Claims rejects a specific land claim made by the Mohawks.
1990	An armed stand-off at Oka lasts for 11 weeks and spreads to the Kahnawake Reserve south of Montreal. The protesters are arrested.
1997	The federal government purchases the disputed land from the town of Oka and gives it to the Mohawk community, formally ending the Oka crisis.

RECONNECT 💡

1. What issues have led to serious Aboriginal protests?

2. How far should Aboriginal peoples go in protesting in your view? Explain clearly.

FOCUS

This section will help you understand
  a. why Aboriginal people want to control their own education
  b. recent changes in the education of Aboriginal students.

The Historical Pattern

In the 100 years following Confederation, the federal government used education as a way of assimilating Aboriginal peoples and eliminating their distinct cultures. In the view of the government, the traditions of many Aboriginal groups had no commercial or military value. Educators in residential and reserve schools especially targeted:

▶ aboriginal ceremonies. Many officials perceived these ceremonies as heathen and a waste of time.

▶ aboriginal languages. By forcing children to speak only in English, the government believed children would then lose their sense of identity as Aboriginal people.

As a result of this educational policy, many Aboriginal students were emotionally scarred.

The assimilation policy underlying Aboriginal education was laid out explicitly in the federal government's White Paper of 1969. Aboriginal groups strongly objected to this document and increased their push for more control of their lives, especially

Figure 26-1 At the Chehalis Community School in the village of Chehalis, British Columbia, students are taught the Salish language Halq'emeylem from kindergarten onwards. The curriculum also includes cultural studies involving traditional beadwork designs and dance ceremonies using traditional costumes.

in education. Since the early 1970s, more and more First Nations have begun to operate schools. By 1996, the number of band-operated schools had risen to 429 (from 64 in 1977). These schools were educating more than half the children living on reserves, and 75 % of students were remaining until Grade 12. As well, the number of Registered Indians and Inuit attending post-secondary institutions had risen to 26 305 (from only 321 in 1970).

Despite these signs of progress, the proportion of Aboriginal students completing high school and attending university remains lower than Canadian national averages.

Improving Education

The experience of First Nations students at off-reserve provincial schools can be difficult. Students often face racism in non-Aboriginal communities and, if separated from their families to attend school, suffer homesickness. The curriculum taught has limited Aboriginal content, and school materials and policies may contain unintended bias against Aboriginal students.

Many provinces and school boards have worked to reduce or eliminate these problems. The Vancouver School District employs First Nations support workers to assist the 2000 Aboriginal students in the area and has special programs for Aboriginal street kids. Saskatchewan has adopted a plan to recruit more Aboriginal teachers, involve more Aboriginal parents, and put more Aboriginal content into the curriculum at school boards where Aboriginal students are at least 5% of the student population. In both Vancouver and Saskatchewan, teachers are trained in cross-cultural awareness and alternative approaches for educating Aboriginal children.

Band-operated schools also face the challenge of incorporating Aboriginal knowledge and concepts into the curriculum. Ideally, the school experience should strongly emphasize learning the students' Aboriginal languages and preparing students to make contributions to their communities and nations if they so desire.

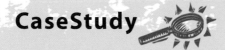

EyeWitness

Colleen McGregor came to the Six Nations Reserve from Kahnawake to teach the Mohawk language at Kawenni:o/Gawenni:yo High School.

"When I heard about the (native language) immersion program, I thought, 'What a great idea.' Most parents of my age lost their language for a number of reasons. I'm really proud of the students here for knowing their culture at such a young age… Most of our young people here do attend our longhouse ceremonies. They take the initiative and they participate fully. I hope it continues, so they can teach the next generation."

CaseStudy

THE AHKWESAHSNE SCIENCE AND MATHEMATICS PILOT PROJECT

In 1988, the Mohawk community of Ahkwesahsne created a novel project to incorporate a Mohawk world view into its mathematics and science curriculum. Mohawk health and science professionals, elders, and parents, as well as non-Aboriginal advisers, created the curriculum for grades seven to nine. The curriculum focuses on the natural world and incorporates the belief that everything in the world is interrelated. It also includes Western science and mathematics concepts.

Figure 26-2 Taryn Thompson (left) and Kayla Point (right) are students in the culturally Integrated Curriculum Project. The project is run by the Ahkwesahsne Mohawk Board of Education, which operates three schools. In addition to a Mohawk-centred curriculum, students play field lacrosse and box lacrosse. Lacrosse is known as "the Creator's game."

Examples of Mohawk-centred lessons include the following:

- Plant study focuses on how plants contribute to Mother Earth, people, and animals; the medicinal uses of plants; the cultural significance of the Three Sisters (corn, beans, and squash); and the Western classification system for plants.

- Animal study includes the animal-based Haudenosaunee clan system used in Mohawk society, as well as cells, cell functions, and the Western classification system for animals.

- Mathematics includes Mohawk number systems and practical applications of numbers to agriculture and forestry.

- Water study includes fieldwork to monitor water quality at the Ahkwesahsne Reserve (located on the St. Lawrence River).

RECONNECT

1. Why is education so vital to Aboriginal communities?

2. Describe two successful improvements in Aboriginal education.

FOCUS

This section will help you understand
a. why changes to the justice system for Aboriginal people are necessary
b. ideas for changing the criminal justice system.

> "There's no such thing as guilt or innocence in Aboriginal justice; there's only the acknowledgement of responsibility."
> —Elizabeth Bellerose, Crown prosecutor of Alberta Cree descent.

A Failing Justice System

In 1991, Aboriginal people in Canada made up only about 3% of the total population, but 11% of the federal inmate population, and 15% of the provincial inmate population. In Manitoba and Saskatchewan, the representation of Aboriginal inmates in provincial jails in 1996 was 49% and 72% respectively.

The Discrimination Factor

Many studies conclude that these disturbing statistics partly result from how the criminal justice system operates. The system, designed by non-Aboriginal people, does not take into account the special circumstances facing many Aboriginal people. The term **systemic discrimination** is used to refer to this problem of the inherent unfairness of the system to a specific group.

The system fails Aboriginal people when it treats them more harshly than non-Aboriginal people and excludes them from the opportunities open to non-Aboriginal people. The following facts have been cited in studies as evidence of systemic discrimination.

▶ Compared to non-Aboriginal people, Aboriginal people are more likely to be placed under surveillance and arrested by police. For example, a 1991 Alberta task force found that Alberta police treated minor offences in public places more strictly if committed by Aboriginal people than if by non-Aboriginal people.

▶ Lawyers spend less time with Aboriginal clients than with non-Aboriginal clients. This is particularly true in isolated communities where lawyers and court personnel fly in to dispense justice.

"IT'S ALL VERY WELL TO ACCUSE THE JUSTICE SYSTEM OF FAILING NATIVES.... BUT WHERE'S YOUR PROOF."

Figure 27-1 How does this cartoon represent the statistics presented above? How does this cartoon misrepresent the statistics?

▶ Aboriginal offenders, due to language and cultural barriers, plead guilty more often than non-Aboriginal offenders. They often plead guilty because of a cultural belief in accepting responsibility—even for something that they did not do. As a result, Aboriginal offenders are more likely to receive prison sentences.

▶ Aboriginal offenders spend a greater proportion of their sentences in prison than non-Aboriginal offenders because they are more reluctant to participate in rehabilitation programs.

▶ Aboriginal offenders have more difficulty obtaining parole. Parole rules often require that offenders stay away from people with criminal records. Aboriginal offenders may come from small reserves where other people have been to prison, and thus they cannot avoid such contact.

Primary Source
THE PEACE AND GOOD ORDER TREATY CLAUSE

All numbered treaties have sections worded similarly to this section from Treaty 6:

> They [the undersigned Chiefs on behalf of their bands] promise and engage that they will in all respects obey and abide by the law, and they will maintain peace and good order between each other,...and that they will aid and assist the officers of Her Majesty in bringing to justice and punishment any Indian offending against the stipulations of this treaty, or infringing the laws in force in the country so ceded.

Some Aboriginal legal scholars have interpreted the last clause of this section as giving chiefs jurisdiction in matters of justice and punishment. With this jurisdiction, they can apply Aboriginal approaches to justice. Other scholars have pointed out a contradiction between maintaining peace and good order and aiding officers of the non-Aboriginal justice system.

The Poverty Factor

Almost one-quarter of all Aboriginal people are unemployed, and 40% of those on reserves receive some sort of social assistance payments. Poor people tend to be over-represented in the criminal justice system for a number of reasons.

► Environments with high levels of unemployment and poverty are known to have higher crime rates than other environments. In such places, it is easier to become involved in criminal activity.

► Lack of money and opportunities can lead people to obtain money illegally.

► Poor people may not be able to afford the best legal representation, and so may have a greater chance of being convicted.

Aboriginal youth living in poverty on reserves, isolated from opportunities and options, are especially vulnerable to involvement in the criminal justice system.

Figure 27-2 Growing up in poverty can be a factor in the over-representation of Aboriginal people in the criminal justice system.

SENTENCED PRISON ADMISSIONS, SELECTED PROVINCES

Province	Rate/10 000 (Aboriginal)	Rate/10 000 (Non-Aboriginal)	Ratio (Aboriginal to Non-Aboriginal)
British Columbia (1991)	106	25	4.24
Alberta (1991)	681	94	7.24
Saskatchewan (1993)	522	21	24.85
Manitoba (1991)	194	20	9.70
Ontario (1991)	115	37	3.10
Average Rate	323	39	8.28

Figure 27-3 Bias in the criminal justice system and social problems result in the over-representation of Aboriginal people in prisons. Significantly, provinces such as Alberta and Saskatchewan use probation less than other regions. What changes to social life and the criminal justice system could reduce this over-representation?

The Cultural Factor

Elders, social workers, and legal scholars have all pointed out that Aboriginal views of justice are profoundly different from the Euro-Canadian view. As part of their process of justice, Aboriginal peoples believe that offenders should be healed and integrated into their communities. In a discussion paper, the Community Holistic Circle Healing (CHCH) Program in Manitoba outlined these differences between the Euro-Canadian and Aboriginal view.

These different ways of approaching justice also affect how one judges the wrongfulness of an act in the first place. For example, during the Oka crisis in 1990, the act of taking up arms against the police and government was not wrong in the view of some Mohawks—they were rightfully protecting a traditional Mohawk burial ground from being turned into a golf course.

ABORIGINAL JUSTICE PROCESS	EURO-CANADIAN JUSTICE PROCESS
• consider and right the imbalance (physical, spiritual, mental, and/or emotional) that led to a wrongdoing	• establish that the individual is guilty of a wrongdoing
• consider and correct the external forces that caused the imbalance	• consult outside specialists about the implications of the wrongdoing
• consider and deal with the consequences of the wrongdoing	• punish the wrongdoer to deter others from future wrongdoing

CaseStudy

WILDLIFE LAWS

Most treaties between the federal government and First Nations guarantee Aboriginal people the right to hunt and fish according to their traditional practices. Since the signing of these treaties, federal and provincial governments have passed laws restricting hunting and fishing. These laws restrict such things as when and where hunting and fishing can occur, and which species and how many of them can be hunted or caught. Sometimes governments exempt Aboriginal people from these laws, but not always. Many Aboriginal people say they should not be subject to these restrictions because of their treaty rights. Those Aboriginal people who ignore wildlife laws can get into trouble with the law. Some of the resulting court cases have set important legal **precedents**.

Figure 27-4 Supreme Court rulings have affirmed Aboriginal rights to continue their traditional fishing and hunting practices.

In 1990, the Supreme Court Sparrow Decision affirmed the right of Aboriginal people in Canada to fish for food, cultural, and ceremonial purposes.

In 1996, a B.C. judge ruled on a case involving an Aboriginal defendant who had moved from Ontario (under Treaty 3) to British Columbia (under Treaty 8). The defendant had been charged with killing two deer and an elk calf out of season. The court ruled in favour of the defendant, giving Registered Indians the right to hunt in any and all treaty jurisdictions in Canada. Some non-Aboriginal Canadians opposed the ruling as unfair because they do not enjoy the same right, and they do not want Aboriginal hunters from other regions to exploit the game and fish resources of their region.

Also in 1996, the Supreme Court made a ruling on cases involving the illegal selling of fish. It was affirmed that Aboriginal people have the right to sell or trade fish if they can prove their ancestors did so as an integral part of their culture prior to European contact.

The meaning of the term "right" is very important in these decisions. A right is not a privilege that can be given or taken away. The Aboriginal right to practise traditions involving wildlife resources is based on the existence of these traditions from pre-contact times.

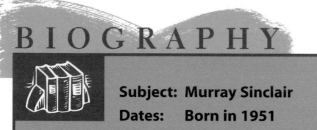

BIOGRAPHY

Subject: Murray Sinclair

Dates: Born in 1951

Most Notable Accomplishment: Manitoba's first Aboriginal judge and co-commissioner of Manitoba's Aboriginal Justice Inquiry.

Thumbnail Sketch: Judge Sinclair and his two brothers and one sister were raised by their grandparents in Selkirk, Manitoba. In 1968, he graduated from the Selkirk Collegiate Institute as athlete of the year and class valedictorian. He planned on becoming a physical education teacher and was one of only a few Aboriginal students enrolled at the time at the University of Manitoba. After two years in the program, he left to look after his grandmother. At 19, while working at the Selkirk Friendship Centre, he was elected vice-president of the Manitoba Métis Federation in the Interlake Region. In 1975, Sinclair was appointed Executive Assistant to Howard Pawley, Manitoba's attorney-general at the time, who influenced him to enroll in the University of Manitoba law school in 1976.

Murray Sinclair's law practice was successful, and in 1988 he was appointed Associate Chief Judge of the Manitoba Provincial Court. With Associate Chief Justice A.C. Hamilton, Judge Sinclair served as co-commissioner of the Public Inquiry into the Administration of Justice and Aboriginal People. Their report, released in 1991, included a powerful discussion of systemic discrimination in Manitoba's justice system and of traditional concepts of Aboriginal justice. The ground-breaking report is included in university law courses throughout the world.

Figure 27-5 Murray Sinclair.

Practising Aboriginal Justice

The focus of many Aboriginal justice traditions is on social harmony rather than on an isolated criminal act. Therefore, improving Canadian legal practices may not be enough to achieve Aboriginal justice. According to many, a truly Aboriginal approach to justice can only be practised within the framework of Aboriginal self-government.

Still, many practical results can be achieved by working to change the Canadian justice system. One change is to involve more Aboriginal people in the system as police officers, translators, court workers, and judges. In 1998, there were 18 Aboriginal judges.

Sentencing circles are a further step that can be taken to improve the system. Participants in the circle include elders and many other community members. Each participant has an equal role in discussing sentencing, and they provide follow-up on the defendant's progress. In these roles they can

Figure 27-6 A Fort Chipewyan, Alberta sentencing circle banished a 19-year-old to live in the bush shown here. He was under his uncle's supervision until space opened up for him in an alcohol treatment program.

help develop and implement improved policies and programs.

RECONNECT

1. Offer three examples of how the Canadian justice system seems unfair to Aboriginal people.

2. Outline your personal views on the use of Aboriginal sentencing circles.

FOCUS 💡

This section will help you understand
  a. the economic conditions of Aboriginal peoples in Canada
  b. the kinds of successful business enterprises launched by Aboriginal peoples.

Aboriginal Peoples and the Economy

Aboriginal peoples as a whole have been less prosperous than non-Aboriginal groups in Canadian society in the 20th century. In fact, since the end of large-scale commercial fur trading in the 19th century, opportunities for Aboriginal people to participate in Canada's economy have been severely limited. As a result, Aboriginal people now experience high levels of unemployment, and many depend on social assistance.

On-Reserve Challenges

Some remote reserves have not developed a sound economic base because they are too small to sustain economic activity. Aboriginal lands south of the 60th parallel—mainly reserves—make up less than 0.5% of the Canadian land mass. Therefore, traditional economic activity cannot be continued, and it is difficult to develop contemporary economic activity.

Resource development in traditional First Nations lands has had mixed economic results. For example, in the 1970s, the giant James Bay hydroelectric project flooded 10 000 square kilometres of Cree and Inuit traditional territory. In compensation, the Cree received $136 million from the Quebec and federal governments under the James Bay and Northern Quebec Agreement signed in

Figure 28-1 Between 1979 and 1982 over 400 wells were drilled within a 25-kilometre radius of the Lubicon community of Little Buffalo.

1975. Despite the creation of successful Aboriginal businesses with this money, unemployment in the region still runs at around 50%.

Resource development is most devastating in cases where Aboriginal people have been following a traditional lifestyle. In the 1980s, oil drilling in the area of the Lubicon Cree band community in Alberta caused the total value of hunting and trapping to fall to 10% of its previous value.

In the 1990s, various initiatives have been taken for First Nations to become co-managers of particular natural resources on their lands. As well, Supreme Court decisions about Aboriginal ownership of traditional lands have led many First Nations to demand payments from resource companies and governments for any resource development.

StatScan Measures of Economic Conditions, 1991

	Labour Force Participation (%)	Unemployment Rates (%)	Recipients of Social Assistance (%)
Total Aboriginal	57.0	24.6	28.6
Registered Indian			
On-reserve	45.3	30.1	41.5
Off-reserve	56.0	29.4	24.8
Non-Registered Indian	67.5	21.1	n/a
Métis	63.7	21.3	22.1
Inuit	57.2	24.1	23.5
Source: The RCAP Report, vol. 3, pp. 168, 170; Vol. 4, p. 14.			

Off-Reserve Challenges

Because they have attained lower levels of education than other Canadians, some Aboriginal people in towns and cities cannot compete for many skilled jobs. The Aboriginal Education Council and the Ministry of Education in Ontario began implementing the Aboriginal Education and Training Strategy in 1992 to increase the participation and completion rates of Aboriginal students at colleges and universities. Their goals include changing post-secondary institutions themselves so that the needs of Aboriginal learners are better met. Another initiative to meet the education challenge is the Aboriginal Business Canada program, founded in 1989. One of its mandates is to develop educational materials for Aboriginal youth who want to own their own businesses. Miziwe Biik—Ojibway for "the gathering of the waters"—is the name of another organization that helps Aboriginal clients upgrade their skills for employment in Toronto. The organization's success rate from 1993 to 1995 was 80%.

Success in Business

There are over 20 000 Aboriginal businesses in Canada. Below are some examples of successful Aboriginal companies in a wide range of fields.

▶ **Forestry**—MLTC Logging and Reforestation Inc., Saskatchewan's largest logging contractor.
▶ **Fishing**—Wabuno Fish Farms on Manitoulin Island, run by the Sucker Creek First Nation, growing rainbow trout.
▶ **Mining**—Torngait Ujaganniavingit Corp. in Labrador, exporting granite to its buyer in Italy.
▶ **Manufacturing**—Asham Curling Supplies, Ltd., in Manitoba, run by Métis entrepreneur Arnold Asham, in business since 1978; Batchewana Band Industries Ltd. and Advanced Thermodynamics Corp. in Ontario, jointly manufacturing heaters, power units, and air conditioners for transport vehicles.
▶ **Transport**—Air Creebec Inc. in Quebec, 100% Cree owned and operated.

▶ **Finance**—Six Nations Community Development Corp. in Ontario, providing $6 million in financing to Aboriginal businesses since 1990.
▶ **Arts and Crafts**—Khot-La-Cha Salish Handicrafts in British Columbia, representing artists all along the West Coast, run by Nancy Nightingale, 1994 runner-up for Canadian Woman Entrepreneur of the Year.
▶ **Food**—Parenteau's Saskatoon Berry Chocolates, Inc., specializing in Canadian gourmet food products, run by Métis entrepreneurs Rodney and Colleen Parenteau.
▶ **Fashion**—Patricia Piché Contemporary Fashion Design, creating custom Aboriginal western wear, run by Patricia Piché, of Cree and Chipewyan descent.
▶ **Computer Hardware and Software**—ACR Systems Inc. in British Columbia, manufacturer of pocket-sized data loggers, invented by Métis Cree company founder Albert Rock, used by NASA, the European Space Agency, the Japanese Red Cross, and others, as well as in Formula One racing cars; Abenaki Associates Inc. in Ontario, customizing accounting software for Aboriginal communities and training computer users, founded by Mi'kmaq Percy Barnaby, Carol Ann Barnaby of Ojibwa descent, and Michelle Poirier.

Figure 28-2 Albert Rock launched ACR Systems in 1985.

RECONNECT

1. Why have many Aboriginal peoples generally not shared in Canada's great economic progress?
2. Identify three Aboriginal business success stories.

FOCUS 🔆

This section will help you understand
a. the implications of the "baby boom" in Aboriginal communities
b. the difficulties of Aboriginal population research.

An Aboriginal "Baby Boom"

In the 1996 Census, about 800 000 people, or 3% of the Canadian population, identified themselves as "North American Indian, Métis or Inuit." The census revealed 554 000 North American Indians, 210 000 Métis, and 41 000 Inuit. Aboriginal populations are growing rapidly, much more rapidly than the Canadian population as a whole. Other statistics from the census showed that Aboriginal people are experiencing a "baby boom." For example,

► the average age in the Aboriginal population was 25.5 years, 10 years younger than the average age in the general Canadian population.

► there were 491 Aboriginal children under 5 years of age for every 1000 Aboriginal women of child-bearing age, as compared to 290 per 1000 in the general Canadian population.

► children under 15 made up 35% of the Aboriginal population, but only 20% of the general Canadian population.

Population Issues

One of the most serious issues surrounding Aboriginal population growth is the availability of reserve housing. If more houses are not built on reserves, many people will need to move into towns and cities. As a result, the problems for Aboriginal people of living in urban centres—**alienation**, threats to culture, loss of language—will affect greater numbers of people. Current population trends also signal the need for more schools and more jobs in Aboriginal communities.

Other statistics from the 1996 Census show that the rate of poverty among Aboriginal people will likely remain high. In Canada, one-parent families tend to be poorer than two-parent families. About one-third of Aboriginal children live in one-parent families, twice the rate for the general population. In urban areas, nearly one-half of Aboriginal children live in one-parent families.

Figure 29-1 The average age of the Aboriginal population is ten years younger than the average age for the general Canadian population. The Aboriginal population is also experiencing a mini "baby boom."

StatScan   Population Distribution, 1996

	Aboriginal Population (rounded to nearest '000)	Aboriginal Population as % of Total Cdn. Pop.	Geographical Distribution of Total Aboriginal Pop. %
Canada	**799 000**	**2.8**	**100.0**
Newfoundland	14 000	2.6	1.8
P.E.I.	1 000	0.7	0.1
Nova Scotia	12 000	1.4	1.5
New Brunswick	10 000	1.4	1.3
Quebec	71 000	1.0	8.9
Ontario	142 000	1.3	17.7
Manitoba	128 000	11.7	16.1
Saskatchewan	111 000	11.4	13.9
Alberta	123 000	4.6	15.4
British Columbia	140 000	3.8	17.5
Yukon Territory	6 000	20.1	0.8
Northwest Territories	40 000	61.9	5.0

In 1996, about 30% of Aboriginal people lived on rural reserves, 50% lived in cities and towns, and 20% lived in rural areas other than reserves.

Source: Statistics Canada, 1996 Census: Aboriginal Data.

Figure 29-2   Which province or territory has the largest number of Aboriginal people? In which province or territory do Aboriginal people form a majority of the population? What percentage of the total Aboriginal population lives east of Manitoba?

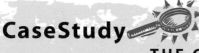

CaseStudy

THE CHALLENGES OF POPULATION STUDY

The number of Status Indians and Inuit can be specified because members of these groups are registered by the federal government. The total number of Aboriginal people in Canada, however, is difficult to determine. One reason is that some Aboriginal bands choose not to participate in the census in order to assert their independence from Canada. Another reason has to do with the wording of the census questionnaire. In response to the 1991 Census question asking Canadians about "cultural origins or ancestry," about 1 million people claimed to *have* Aboriginal ancestry. In response to the 1991 Aboriginal Peoples Survey, however, only 626 000 people *identified with* their Aboriginal ancestry. In other words, less than two-thirds of the people who said they had Aboriginal ancestry identified with it.

Obviously, more Canadians have Aboriginal ancestry than identify themselves as Aboriginal. Possibly, some of these people have been assimilated. Or, perhaps they have been reluctant to acknowledge their Aboriginal heritage. It may be that these people will rediscover their traditions and acknowledge their Aboriginal ancestry in the future.

In 1996, as in 1991, Aboriginal people accounted for between 2 and 4% of Canada's total population, depending on whether statisticians used Aboriginal identity or Aboriginal ancestry to represent the Aboriginal population. A total of 76 reserves refused to participate in the 1996 Census. There are about 2300 reserves in Canada.

17. To which ethnic or cultural group(s) did this
■ person's **ancestors** belong?

For example, French, English, German, Scottish, Canadian, Italian, Irish, Chinese, Cree, Micmac, Métis, Inuit (Eskimo), Ukranian, Dutch, East Indian, Polish, Portuguese, Jewish, Haitian, Jamaican, Vietnamese, Lebanese, Chilean, Somali, etc.

18. Is this person an Aboriginal person, that is,
■ North American Indian, Métis or Inuit (Eskimo)?

If "Yes", mark the circle(s) that best describe(s) this person now.

Figure 29-3   These questions, numbers 17 and 18 from the 1996 Census, deal with Aboriginal identity and ancestry.

RECONNECT

1. What is the "Aboriginal baby boom" and why is it significant?

2. Why is it so difficult to get an accurate "count" of Canada's Aboriginal population?

FOCUS

This section will help you understand
a. why Aboriginal people move to cities
b. the challenges Aboriginal people face in cities.

> **There is a strong, sometimes racist, perception that being Aboriginal and being urban are mutually exclusive.**
> — Native Council of Canada.

From the Reserve to the City

During the 1950s, while many Canadians were moving from inner cities to suburbs, Status Indians began leaving their reserves for cities and towns. Now, fewer than 60% of Registered Indians, and only 35 % of the total Aboriginal population, live on reserves. Since 1966, the number of off-reserve Status Indians has increased by about 300%.

There are many reasons why some Aboriginal people feel compelled to leave.
▶ It is difficult to find work on reserves that are small and isolated.
▶ Some reserves have many social problems, such as drug and alcohol abuse, political infighting, and poor and overcrowded housing.
▶ Some Aboriginal women and youths seek to escape physical and sexual abuse.
▶ Many young people go to attend school, college, or university.
▶ To some, the city has the appealing image of an exciting place to be.

Isolation

To leave a reserve for the city is a serious decision. It often means losing connections to family, the community and the land. This loss can be devastating. For many Aboriginal people, connection to the land is an essential part of who they are and gives them a way of understanding how they fit into the world. Separation from family and community also makes it harder to maintain Aboriginal languages and culture.

Aboriginal friendship centres across Canada help Aboriginal people living in cities maintain their cultural identities. These centres employ elders who teach knowledge of traditions and ceremonies, as well as Aboriginal languages. The centres also allow Aboriginal people to meet with each other, and provide a focus for health, employment, and other community services.

Poverty

Aboriginal people often encounter racism and closed doors when they look for jobs in cities. They suffer from unemployment at a rate two to three times higher than non-Aboriginal people. Poverty results. In 1991, more than 60% of the Aboriginal households living in Winnipeg, Regina, and Saskatoon had incomes below the poverty line (the amount of money below which a person or family is considered poor.)

Figure 30-1 Aboriginal friendship centres like this one help Aboriginal people moving into cities maintain their cultural identities and adjust to the change in environment.

EyeWitness

In Volume 4 of the 1996 RCAP Report, Aboriginal individuals are quoted describing their lives in the city.

I think the most terrible experience for an Indian person in the urban setting is racism in the community. That diminishes your self-esteem, confidence, and everything else. You experience racism every day in the stores and everywhere else on the street. All the other groups discriminate against you.

You're not only learning there are differences, but you are building your identity on who you are and what you are. And either you turn against your culture and deny that you're Indian and try to assimilate, or you can accept that you're Indian and you can still live in the city and...be a stronger person for it.

I think I've learned to maintain a sense of balance. Because I've adjusted to the European way of doing things in terms of working for money but at the same time maintaining my heritage. Even though it is difficult, because in the urban setting we don't practice a lot of our ceremonial part of our heritage. So my job helps me get back home to that.

—RCAP Report, 1996, Vol. 4, ch. 7, pp. 6, 8, 10.

CaseStudy

ABORIGINAL PEOPLE IN VANCOUVER

According to the 1991 Census, there were a total of 13 360 people with Aboriginal origins or First Nations registration among Vancouver's population of 471 844. The United Native Nations Society, however, estimated the far greater figure of up to 60 000 First Nations people in the Greater Vancouver area. That number can only increase dramatically in the future, given present trends. In the 20 years between 1976 and 1996, the proportion of the total Aboriginal population of B.C. living on reserves had dropped from 63.9% to 49.7%. The proportion of those living off-reserve had risen to 50.3% from 36.1%.

The off-reserve group face many challenges. According to a 1994 Premier's Office report, 26% of the province's off-reserve First Nations people are jobless; 13% cite discrimination as the reason why they cannot find work.

Since 1943, the Vancouver Aboriginal Friendship Centre Society (VAFCS) has been providing support for urban Aboriginals. Today, VAFCS offers several programs and facilities to deal with the challenges of city life, including:

- the Aries Project—support, counselling, and training for street youth
- the Judge Alfred Scow Gymnasium
- the Sundance Daycare Centre—integrated to include special needs children
- the CAPC Program—A Community Action Program— for families with young children who are at risk
- the Aboriginal Head Start Program—for preschoolers
- Young Parents' Support Services
- Fetal Alcohol Syndrome Counselling and Training
- a Chef/Cook Training Program
- the Elderspeak Wisdom Council—amalgamating various elders' groups.

As well, VAFCS operates the Cedar Roots Gallery, a store selling Aboriginal artifacts and gift items.

Figure 30-2 The Vancouver Aboriginal Friendship Centre. Vancouver's Centre is one of the three largest in the province.

RECONNECT

1. Describe the major challenges facing Aboriginal people who move from a reserve to a city.

2. Identify three VAFCS programs which help Aboriginal people adjust more successfully to urban life.

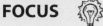
FOCUS

This section will help you understand
a. youth-related issues in the Aboriginal population
b. strategies for improving youth self-esteem and pride.

A Key Population Sector

We saw in Chapter 29 that the Aboriginal community is experiencing a "baby boom." This means that the numbers of Aboriginal youth are increasing. How this sector of the population fares will be key to the future of Aboriginal peoples.

Young people generally face many challenges as they undergo the changes of adolescence. Factors such as the following are responsible for depression among young people, and can even lead to youth suicide:

▶ family instability or dysfunction.

▶ history of sexual abuse or of prolonged or unresolved grief.

▶ substance abuse involving alcohol, drugs, or gas sniffing.

▶ poverty.

▶ feelings of worthlessness.

▶ loss of traditional culture and the breakdown of cultural values and rules.

▶ suicide pacts between friends, leading to cluster suicides.

Canada as a whole has the third highest rate of suicide in the world for youths 15 to 19 years of age.

Unfortunately, many of the most common reasons for suicide are compounded in Aboriginal families and communities. The suicide rate for Aboriginal people as a whole is about three times as high as that for the Canadian population. A study from the early 1990s showed that, among the Status Indian population, girls aged 10 to 19 were 8 times more likely to die from suicide than non-Aboriginal girls. Also, boys in the same age range were 4.7 times more likely to die from suicide than non-Aboriginal boys.

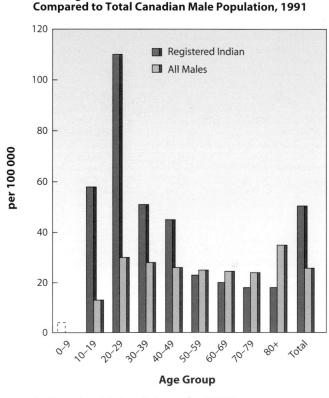

(Suicide rates for male Registered Indians runs from 1987-1991.
Excludes N.W.T. and Pacific region.)

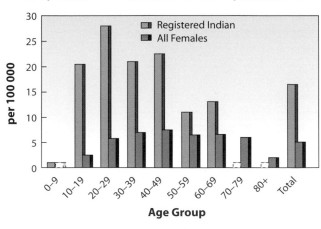

(Suicide rates for female Registered Indians runs from 1987-1991.
Excludes N.W.T. and Pacific region.)

Figure 31-1 These graphs shows that the Aboriginal youth suicide rate is much higher than that of the general youth population of Canada.

The case of Ushimassit (Davis Inlet) shows how some of these factors converged to produce tragedy. In 1967, the governments of Canada and Newfoundland convinced the Innu to move from their traditional lands to the island village of Davis Inlet. The new community was cut off from the mainland and traditional hunting grounds for up to four months each year, and the town had no roads, no plumbing, and insufficient fresh water. Alcohol became a serious problem, and between 1973 and 1993, 47 people died alcohol-related deaths—half of them young people under 20 years old. In 1993, the community received worldwide attention when six children tried to commit suicide by sniffing gasoline.

In 1996, the Canadian and Newfoundland governments agreed to move the Innu community to a new mainland location at Sango Pond. The governments will spend $85 million to build a larger community with indoor plumbing, a wharf, and an airstrip.

Strategies For Youth

Many of the recommendations for solving youth problems in the 1996 RCAP Report involves education. They included:
- ▶ the creation of a national Aboriginal youth policy that would address education.
- ▶ an early childhood education program.
- ▶ the creation of an Aboriginal controlled education system.
- ▶ the development of Aboriginal curriculum at school boards with large numbers of Aboriginal students.
- ▶ the acknowledgement of traditional arts and culture courses with academic credit.
- ▶ the acknowledgement of elders as paid teachers.
- ▶ the creation of an Aboriginal peoples' international university.

Related to the promotion of education are youth mentoring projects and conferences, such as the National Aboriginal Youth Conference. In Manitoba, youth mentoring takes place both at the

Figure 31-2 In 1997, a group of First Nations, Métis, and Inuit youth produced a documentary video on Aboriginal youth issues entitled *Balance—Healing Through Helping*. It won the "Best Public Service Video" award at the American Indian Film Festival and has been distributed to friendship centres, schools, and youth centres across Canada.

peer level (for example, through the Manitoba Aboriginal Youth Achievement Awards) and from adult to teenager (for example, through the role model program of the Manitoba Aboriginal Youth Career Awareness Committee. Over 100 Aboriginal role models have joined the MAYCAC program, speaking to youth throughout the province about dealing with racism, single parenthood and off-reserve life. They stress the value of staying in school at least until Grade 12, and also of learning the traditional teachings of elders.

Spiritual growth through traditional values is the most demanding and powerful solution to Aboriginal youth problems. Young people in Davis Inlet have looked to this solution in their dramatic productions. The Innu Theater Company has presented several plays that dramatize the conflict between Aboriginal spiritual values and Euro-Canadian culture. Such productions have had a strong impact on the community.

NETSURFER

www.innu.ca

The Web site of the Innu Nation has an excellent collection of documents on Innu history. The site also has information on contemporary political and economic issues and social issues affecting women and youth. It is updated regularly.

RECONNECT

1. State three reasons why young people in general, and Aboriginal youth in particular, suffer from depression.

2. In your opinion, which of the strategies for youth noted in this chapter would likely be most successful? Why?

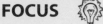

FOCUS

This section will help you understand
   a. the challenges and achievements of Aboriginal women in the working world
   b. the role of Aboriginal women in politics.

Aboriginal Women and Work

Traditionally, women played a variety of roles within Aboriginal communities. For example, Ojibwa women were responsible for household cooking, sewing, and child care, as well as: weaving fish nets; paddling the canoe during the duck hunt; making protective robes; building the roofs of wigwams; tanning hides; and harvesting rice and maple syrup. In addition, women had the role of advisers in many communities. In some nations, women were the exclusive owners of homes, tools and implements, and products of subsistence activities such as farming.

In the present-day wage labour market, Aboriginal women have not been quite as successful. In general, they work less and earn less than both Aboriginal men and Canadians as a whole. Wage labour, however, is not the only concern of Aboriginal women, especially those coping with inequality and violence in their families and bands as well as in the larger society. As

Figure 32-1 Cornelia Wieman is the first Aboriginal woman to become a psychiatrist. In 1998, she finished her residency at McMaster University Medical Centre and became a fellow of the Royal College of Physicians and Surgeons of Canada.

Mohawk Professor Patricia Monture-Angus pointed out at the 1997 Forging a New Relationship conference, "Healing is... hard work. Unfortunately, healing has become women's work and, like women, has been marginalized."

StatScan   Labour Data for Aboriginal Women, 1991

- Only half of adult Aboriginal women participated in the labour market, compared to nearly three-quarters of Aboriginal men.
- The unemployment rate of Aboriginal women was twice as high as the national rate.
- Their average total income was $11 897, which represented about 70% of the average of Aboriginal men.
- The Yukon had the highest proportion of Registered Indian females in the labour force, at 64%.
- Saskatchewan had the lowest proportion, at 29%.
- Aboriginal women owned 6935 businesses, which represented about 37% of the total 18 625 Aboriginal-owned businesses.
- In 1993, 6% of the female Aboriginal labour force were self-employed, compared to 9.9% of the total Canadian female labour force, 9.9% of the male Aboriginal labour force, and 13.3% of the total Canadian labour force of both sexes.
- In both 1993/94 and 1994/95, First Nations women outnumbered First Nations men nearly two to one in post-secondary enrolment.

Sources: The 1991 Aboriginal Peoples Survey; INAC Customized Data, Based on 1991 Census of Population; Entrepreneurship & Small Business Office, Industry & Science Canada, 1993; Facts from Stats, Issue 9 (Dec-Jan 1996), Information Quality and Research Directorate, Information Management Branch, DIAND.

Political Challenges and Achievements

During the 1992 constitutional talks leading to the Charlottetown Accord, the Native Women's Association of Canada (NWAC) was concerned that the rights of Aboriginal women, then protected by the Charter of Rights and Freedoms, could be

Figure 32-2 In 1992, NWAC members demanded protection of Aboriginal women's rights under the proposal for Aboriginal self-government in the Charlottetown Accord.

Figure 32-3 Aboriginal women are underrepresented in band leadership. Several women, however, have achieved leadership positions. For example, Wendy Grant-John served three terms as chief of the Musqueam Nation in Vancouver and ran for the position of national chief of the Assembly of First Nations. In 1998 she was working for DIAND as an associate regional director.

lost under Aboriginal self-government. NWAC had not been invited to the negotiations, although four other Aboriginal organizations had been. When NWAC demanded a hearing, it was ignored. NWAC then launched a court case to win a place at the negotiating table, but was unsuccessful.

Aboriginal women's groups continue to press their issues as the political status of Aboriginal people evolves. The 1996 RCAP Report stated that women identified four major areas of concern:
▶ the Indian Act and the impact of Bill C-31's amendments,
▶ the need for healing through health and social service programs,
▶ the vulnerability of women and children to violence, and
▶ accountability and fairness in self-government.

While women have lost their pre-contact power and status in many First Nations, they have maintained their long-standing roles in Mohawk communities, traditionally within the Haudenosaunee (Iroquois) Confederacy. Following the Great Law, adopted over six hundred years ago, each clan in the Confederacy is represented by a clan mother. Each woman in a clan votes to determine which male clan member will become chief. If the women in the clan believe the chosen chief is acting inappropriately, they can replace him. At times, these traditional chiefs and the women who support them have come into conflict with the officially recognized band chief and council.

In the 1990s, the Nunavut Implementation Commission (NIC) sought ways to help Nunavut regain the balance between women and men that was traditional to Inuit culture. It recommended gender equality—each constituency in the legislative assembly to be represented by a woman and a man. The proposal, however, was rejected by Nunavut voters in 1997.

RECONNECT

1. Why were women vital to the success of traditional Aboriginal communities?

2. Briefly describe two major challenges facing Aboriginal women today?

FOCUS

This section will help you understand
a. the history of Aboriginal health issues
b. current health problems and strategies for treatment.

A Legacy of Disease

Europeans brought infectious diseases such as smallpox and measles to North America. Many historians estimate that such diseases killed 80 to 90% of the total Aboriginal population of the continent. Fatal outbreaks of disease continued into the 20th century. In fact, after declining for 400 years, the number of Aboriginal people in Canada only started to increase after 1910.

Health Problems Today

While the population growth rate of Aboriginal people is now higher than that of other Canadians, their state of health is often much worse. On average, Aboriginal people have shorter life expectancy for both men and women, higher infant mortality, higher rates of accidental and violent deaths, and higher incidences of diseases such as tuberculosis and diabetes. Many of these health patterns can be traced to social problems such as poverty, poor housing, and substance abuse.

In 1990, poverty was a reality for 28.6% of Aboriginal people over the age of 15 who relied on social assistance for at least part of their income. Only 8.1% of the total Canadian population are in this category. As well, the unemployment rate for Aboriginal people is two to three times as high as for non-Aboriginal people. Pregnant women suffering from poverty are more likely to have low birthweight babies. These babies are more likely to die in infancy or to experience chronic health problems. Poor children are more likely to suffer from poor nutrition and to live in unsafe environments.

Insufficient housing on reserves leads to overcrowding. Overcrowding and poor sanitation lead to health problems such as communicable diseases and skin infections. In 1991, 11.5% of reserve houses had no bathrooms, 19.4% did not have a flush toilet, 24% did not have water suitable for drinking,

Figure 33-1 A few years after this picture was taken in the village of Yan in 1881, smallpox ravaged the community and the survivors moved to Masset, British Columbia.

and 6.5% did not have electricity. Compared to other Canadians, people on reserves were ninety times more likely to live in houses that lacked piped water, three times more likely to live in houses without central heating, and ten times more likely to live in houses without flush toilets.

According to the Canadian Centre on Substance Abuse, Aboriginal people suffer from alcohol psychosis at four times the national average rate, and from liver disease (a problem connected with alcohol consumption) at over three times the national average rate. Aboriginal people also make up one-fifth of all hospital admissions for alcohol-related illnesses. Alcohol abuse is associated with many injuries and deaths, as well as fetal alcohol syndrome (fetuses exposed to alcohol can develop permanent brain damage).

The 1996 RCAP Report stressed the need for Aboriginal healing centres that would address the physical, psychological, and spiritual health of Aboriginal peoples.

Holistic Healing

The RCAP Report also stated that equal access of Aboriginal people to medical care is not enough to ensure health. Rather, governments must commit to "rough equality of outcomes in health status." Many Aboriginal people stress that such outcomes can only be achieved by incorporating traditional approaches to medicine into Aboriginal health care.

In many Aboriginal traditions, the medicine wheel is seen as the foundation for health and well-being. The medicine wheel is a symbol of wholeness and vitality and teaches the need for balancing the physical, mental, emotional, and spiritual aspects of human nature.

The Stoney Rerserve in southwestern Alberta is one of the many communities that seeks to apply a traditional **holistic** approach to healing and community well being. The reserve's Self-Improvement Through Empowerment (S.I.T.E.) program uses personal-growth workshops to help residents care for their bodies, think rationally and positively, express their feelings honestly, and develop spiritual relationships. The program has helped many people successfully fight depression, negativity, and dependence.

Age-old purification ceremonies such as the sweat lodge continue to cleanse the souls and bodies of participants. The sweat lodge ceremony, encompassing the four sacred elements of earth, water, air, and fire, taps into deep sources of energy through prayer and rounds of sweating in intense heat.

Hospitals are increasingly seeing the need for Aboriginal health services programs. In such programs, patients may ask for the ceremonial burning of traditional medicines such as sweet grass or tobacco.

EyeWitness

Inuit Values in Health Care

In 1996, Dr. Gail Gray spent a week on Baffin Island on a retreat devoted to discussions about health care delivery in the North.

"As Inuit values and customs traditionally have been passed from one generation to another by word of mouth, each elder had stories to tell of community and personal healing practices.

One told of a treatment for boils…

Traditional cures for sore joints include the topical application of green algae from river rocks, or warming the affected area with small rocks heated in fires…

Both men and women in the community gather the plants and mosses used to heal various ailments.…

The community also deals regularly with mental-health problems and social issues. Individual interventions, often provided with the help of a shaman or respected elder, are done discreetly to avoid hurtful gossip and to preserve the stability of the community. Emotional and spiritual wellness is promoted by a strict set of rules that governs the behaviour of each person and establishes each individual's relationship with the community. The importance of family, both for personal and community integrity, was emphasized.

…Love of the land, the importance of relationships, respect for elders—such values must underlie any health care initiatives and be intrinsic in any new programs…"

—Dr. Gail Gray, "Health care in North must acknowledge Inuit values, traditional medicine," in *Canadian Medical Association Journal* 1996; 155: 1613-1614.

RECONNECT

1. Identify five serious health problems facing many Aboriginal peoples today.

2. In your view, which of the above problems is most serious? Why?

3. Describe three traditional Aboriginal health practices being revived today.

FOCUS 💡

This section will help you understand
a. how the achievements of Aboriginal peoples are being recognized.

A Decade of Recognition

In the 1990s, ways of honouring Aboriginal achievements have included the North American Indigenous Games (begun in 1990), the National Aboriginal Achievement Awards (NAAA; begun in 1994), and National Aboriginal Day (instituted in 1996). National Aboriginal Day, on June 21, also supports the United Nations International Decade of the World's Indigenous People, running from 1995 to 2004. The same sense of cultural rebirth that these events help to foster has taken place in the lives of many Aboriginal individuals who have been awarded special recognition.

BIOGRAPHY

Subject: Douglas Cardinal

Dates: Born in 1934

Most Notable Accomplishment: Designed the Canadian Museum of Civilization (CMC) in Hull, Quebec.

Figure 34-1 Douglas Cardinal.

Thumbnail Sketch: Cardinal is the eldest of eight children born to Joseph Cardinal, a part Siksika fish-and-wildlife warden, and Francis, a Métis-German nurse. Due to his mother's poor health when he was 10, he was sent to a Catholic convent school in Red Deer, Alberta, where he first encountered architecture through books. After graduation, he studied architecture at the University of British Columbia and the University of Texas at Austin. Between 1963 and 1985, his commissions included St. Mary's Catholic Church in Red Deer, Grand Prairie Regional College, the Edmonton Space Sciences Centre, and St. Albert Place. In his mid-thirties, Cardinal underwent a deep spiritual change when he was challenged by both Aboriginal and non-Aboriginal leaders to acknowledge his heritage. He participated in sweat lodges, studied under a medicine man, and designed many Aboriginal schools, halfway houses, and friendship centres. In addition to designing the Museum of Civilization in the 1990s, he has developed a master plan for a Cree community in northern Quebec. The United Nations selected this design, which uses traditional Cree cultural values, as one of 50 communities in the world that best reflects the objectives of the UN.

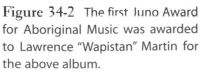

Figure 34-2 The first Juno Award for Aboriginal Music was awarded to Lawrence "Wapistan" Martin for the above album.

Figure 34-3 The 1996 Juno winner was the group Jerry Alfred & the Medicine Beat. On the album Alfred sings in Northern Tutchone.

Figure 34-4 In 1998, Buffy Sainte-Marie was the NAAA Lifetime Achievement winner.

BIOGRAPHY

Subject: Olive Dickason

Dates: Born in 1926

Most Notable Accomplishment: Her book, *Canada's First Nations*, completed when she was in her seventies, is one of the foremost texts on the history of Aboriginal peoples in Canada.

Thumbnail Sketch: Dickason was born in Winnipeg, where she attended an Oblate college until Grade 8. When her father, an English banker, was financially wiped out in the Depression, the family moved to the bush where her Métis mother taught them the survival skills they needed. After a stint selling door-to-door magazine subscriptions at 19, Dickason met up with Father Athol Murray in Saskatchewan, who helped her get a B.A. from Notre Dame College/ University of Ottawa. For the next 24 years, Dickason worked as a successful journalist at major Canadian newspapers. Well into her forties, Dickason reached a turning point in her life where she rediscovered her Aboriginal heritage and wanted to study it. Unfortunately, universities at the time did not recognize Aboriginal history as an academic discipline. With help from broad-minded professors, Dickason earned her Master's degree in Mi'kmaq history when she was 55. Her PhD thesis, *Myth of the Savage*, was published by the press at the University of Alberta, where Dickason took up a teaching post. A few short years later, she was forced to retire at 65. Over the next seven years, she waged a court battle against mandatory retirement and worked on the book *Canada's First Nations*. When she was 72, the landmark book was published and the Supreme Court decided against her case. In 1996, Dickason received the Order of Canada and completed revisions for the fourth edition of *Canada's First Nations*.

Figure 34-5
Olive Dickason.

TECHLINK

COMPUTERS TO CULTURE

"On an airplane, my Powerbook is singing to me in Lakota, while the words to the song appear onscreen in both Lakota and English.

In the Canadian Rockies, Indians carrying portable computers trudge through a herd of elk and into the Banff Centre for the Arts where the 'Drumbeats to Drumbytes' thinktank confronts the reality of online life as it affects Native artists…

Across Canada, thousands of First Nations children network their observations and life experiences into mainstream education, as the Cradleboard Teaching Project—Kids From Kanata partnership provides both Native content and connectivity to schools as far away as Hawaii and Baffin Island.

I make a commercial record in a tipi on the Saskatchewan plains, and CBC television films the event for international broadcast…

…The reality of the situation is that we're not all dead and stuffed in some museum with the dinosaurs: we are Here in this digital age. We have led the pack in a couple of areas (digital music and online art). Although our potential at the moment exceeds the extensiveness of our community computer usage, our projects are already bearing fruit, we expect to prosper and to contribute, and we will defend our data.

…If I have a message in this scant overview, it is this: real Indian people are rising to the potential of the technology, in school and out. We were born for this moment and we are solidly behind our pathfinders."

—Buffy Sainte-Marie, quoted from "CyberSkins: Live and Interactive," http://www.cradleboard.org/cyber.htm ©1997, Buffy Sainte-Marie.

RECONNECT

1. Identify three ways in which Aboriginal people's success is recognized in Canada.

2. According to Buffy Sainte-Marie, how can technology help Aboriginal people? Do you agree? Explain.

FOCUS 💡

This section will help you understand
   a. the positive changes in the representation of Aboriginal people in media.

Control of Media

Mainstream Canadian media and Hollywood movies have misrepresented Aboriginal people in the past. For most of the 20th century, movies have most often depicted Aboriginal people in battle as the antagonists killing white-skinned heroes. The setting for these movies has been the "Wild West," which had to be "tamed" by eliminating the land's First Nations.

Taking control of many different types of media has been an important step for Aboriginal people in correcting this misrepresentation. Today, Aboriginal programming on radio and television is combatting **stereotypes** while it is reinvigorating Aboriginal languages. Inuit programming began with radio in the 1960s and expanded to television in the 1980s with the creation of the Inuit Broadcasting Corporation. In movies, it is no longer acceptable for non-Aboriginal actors to play Aboriginal characters.

Aboriginal movie stars, performing in non-stereotypical roles, include Graham Greene and Tantoo Cardinal. Greene achieved fame playing a Lakota Sioux in *Dances With Wolves*. He has also starred in films such as *The Education of Little Tree*, *Thunderheart*, *Die Hard With a Vengeance*, *Medicine River*, and *Clearcut*. Tantoo Cardinal may still be best known for her role as Blackshawl in *Dances With Wolves*, but she has a long list of acclaimed performances in films such as *Smoke Signals*, *The Education of Little Tree*, *Legends of the Fall*, *Where the Rivers Flow North* and *Black Robe*. In interviews Cardinal has spoken of the need for Aboriginal women to be cast as doctors, lawyers, and other less traditional, contemporary roles.

Alanis Obomsawin and Gil Cardinal are among a growing number of Aboriginal filmmaker/directors whose documentaries have earned national and

BIOGRAPHY

Subject: Tom Jackson

Dates: Born in Saskatchewan in 1948

Most Notable Accomplishment: His Huron Carole concert tour has raised more than $375 000 for food banks, while his starring role as Lynx River Chief Peter Kenidi in the CBC TV series *North of 60* is critically acclaimed.

Thumbnail Sketch: Jackson began acting in his twenties, after spending some years living on the streets in Winnipeg in search of adventure and experience. By 1987, he had moved to Toronto to pursue his acting career. Still living a somewhat rough-edged life in the city, Jackson was moved one night at seeing an elderly man unconscious and lying on the sidewalk, being ignored by passersby. After getting help for the man, Jackson committed himself to helping others on a long-term basis. He organized the first Huron Carole Benefit Concert for an Aboriginal food bank. The annual fundraising tour is now over ten years old. Throughout this time, Jackson has been acting (on *Star Trek: The Next Generation, Street Legal, North of 60*, among other shows and films) and singing (the albums *No Regrets* and *That Side of the Window* were released in 1995 and 1996 respectively). Jackson has received numerous nominations and awards for acting, music recording, and community service.

Figure 35-1
Tom Jackson.

international acclaim. Obomsawin has documented many issues and events in her 30-year career, including the Oka crisis and its aftermath (*Kanehsatake:270 Years of Resistance* and *Spudwrench Kahnawake Man*), police raids on a Mi'kmaq reserve (*Incident Restigouche*), alcoholic recovery (*Poundmaker's Lodge*), and the problems of Aboriginal youth (*Richard Cardinal: Cry from the Diary of a Métis Child* and *No Address*). Cardinal's film topics have included fetal alcohol syndrome (*David with F.A.S.*), child welfare systems, both Aboriginal and non-Aboriginal (*Tikinagan* and *Foster Child*), and Aboriginal spirituality programs in correctional institutions (*The Spirit Within*).

Increasingly, Aboriginal people are winning a more realistic image in the national media. Racist, biased and ethnocentric views are finally being replaced with fair, honest portrayals of the triumphs and tragedies of Aboriginal history and life.

Figure 35-2 In its first six seasons, *North of 60* drew an average weekly audience of 1 million English Canadians, was seen in 60 countries and territories around the world, and was dubbed into more than ten different languages. The series has won several Gemini and other awards and is widely watched in Aboriginal communities across Canada. It is about the small town of Lynx River in Canada's North and follows the lives of an Aboriginal RCMP officer, her brother and band chief, and the former town nurse.

Figure 35-3   The major television event of CBC Television's 1998 – 99 schedule was *Big Bear*, a four-hour miniseries about the struggle of Plains Cree Chief Big Bear to negotiate a better treaty for his people, given the inevitability of the loss of their traditional way of life. The story is told from the Aboriginal point of view and is directed, produced, and co-written by Aboriginal people, with Aboriginal actors in all the starring roles. From left to right: Kennetch Charlette, Gordon Tootosis, Lorne Cardinal, and Michael Obey.

RECONNECT 💡

1. Briefly describe how the "Wild West" image of Aboriginal peoples is being improved in the media today.

FOCUS 💡

This section will help you understand
   a. the common problems facing Indigenous peoples around the world
   b. some of the achievements of Indigenous peoples' groups in the 1990s.

Who Are Indigenous Peoples?

Indigenous peoples are those whose homelands have been overrun by people from other lands. This definition obviously applies to the Aboriginal peoples of North and South America, as well as the Indigenous peoples in Australia and New Zealand. Europeans settled all of those lands hundreds of years ago and dispossessed the original inhabitants. But the definition also applies to Tibetans and Papua New Guineans. These people live in countries only recently overrun by outsiders.

About 300 million people throughout the world qualify as Indigenous peoples. Many have suffered historical experiences similar to those of Canada's Aboriginal peoples. Most continue to experience similar social and legal challenges.

Common Problems

Throughout the world, Indigenous peoples face discrimination from dominant mainstream societies. These societies undervalue Indigenous languages and traditional Indigenous knowledge, displace Indigenous people from their lands, and ignore land claims.

World Distribution of Indigenous Peoples, 1990

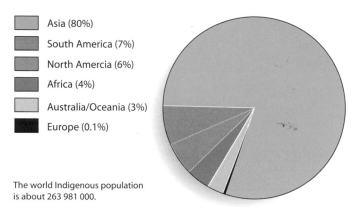

- ▨ Asia (80%)
- ▨ South America (7%)
- ▨ North Amercia (6%)
- ▨ Africa (4%)
- ▨ Australia/Oceania (3%)
- ■ Europe (0.1%)

The world Indigenous population is about 263 981 000.

Figure 36-1 The following countries have Indigenous populations over 5 million: China (87 million); India (70 million); Myanmar (11 million); Mexico (8 million); Peru (8 million); Afghanistan (7 million); Pakistan (7 million); the Philippines (6 million).

EyeWitness

Rigoberta Menchù Tum

In 1992, this Guatemalan leader (b. 1959) became the first Indigenous and the youngest person ever to receive the Nobel Peace Prize. In her acceptance speech she said,

"Among the most bitter dramas that a great percentage of the population has to endure is the forced exodus, which means to be forced by military units and persecution to abandon their villages, their Mother Earth, where their ancestors rest, their environment, the nature that gave them life and the growth of their communities, all of which constitute a coherent system of social organization and functional democracy.

"The case of the displaced and refugees in Guatemala is heartbreaking; some of them are condemned to live in exile in other countries, but the great majority live in exile in their own country. They are forced to wander from place to place, to live in ravines and inhospitable places, some not recognized as Guatemalan citizens, but all of them are condemned to poverty and hunger. There cannot be a real democracy as long as this problem is not satisfactorily solved and these people are reintegrated into their lands and villages."

—Rigoberta Menchù Tum, excerpted from her Nobel Acceptance Speech, December 10, 1992.

For example, the Maoris of New Zealand control only 6% of the land they controlled in 1840, when they signed a treaty guaranteeing them "full, exclusive and undisturbed possession of their lands and estates, forests, fisheries, and other properties."

Mining and logging companies have intruded on traditional lands in countries such as Bangladesh (the Karnaphuli reservoir displaced over 100 000 people); Brazil (the Tucurui and Itaipu dams displaced 50 000); and Canada (the James Bay Hydro Project flooded 10 500 square kilometres and displaced the James Bay Cree from traditional hunting grounds).

As a result of social and economic discrimination, Indigenous peoples tend to have lower life expectancies than non-Indigenous peoples and to suffer from high rates of addiction to alcohol and other substances.

A New Millennium?

Indigenous leaders, such as Rigoberta Menchù Tum, have been fighting against the oppression of their peoples for centuries. Following is a list of some achievements in the 1990s that may make the next millennium more hopeful for many Indigenous groups.

▶ In 1992, Australia's High Court acknowledged Aboriginal title to land and said that Aborigines could seek to reclaim land held by the government. The decision is important but has met with considerable opposition, especially in the province of Western Australia, where up to 40% of the land could be reclaimed.

▶ The UN International Decade of the World's Indigenous People (1995-2004) was adopted to encourage international cooperation in solving the problems facing Indigenous peoples.

▶ In 1996, New Zealand's government agreed to compensate the Ngai Tahu Maori tribe for land lost during the last century, settling a 152-year-old land claim. The deal allowed the Maori to choose from a range of Crown assets, and is worth $170 million. The Crown's formal settlement offer in 1997 also included an apology and the return of the country's highest mountain to the Ngai Tahu, to be renamed "Aoraki/Mount Cook," with the Maori name preceding the European name.

▶ In 1998, work was begun on the creation of a global university for Indigenous peoples on the Internet. Canada's Saskatchewan Indian Federated College, universities in Mexico, and universities in Chile are currently developing curriculum, with negotiations under way for the participation of Australia, Guatemala, and Ecuador.

Primary Source

THE RIGHTS OF INDIGENOUS PEOPLES

One of the goals of the International Decade of the World's Indigenous People is to achieve the UN adoption of a Declaration on Indigenous Peoples' Rights. Work on a Draft Declaration was begun in 1985 by the Working Group on Indigenous Populations. By the 1997 session, two of the Draft's 45 articles had been passed: Article 5 and Article 43.

Article 3 (point of contention)
Indigenous peoples have the right to self-determination. By virtue of that right they freely determine their political status and freely pursue their economic, social and cultural development.

Article 5
Every indigenous individual has the right to a nationality.

Article 43
All the rights and freedoms recognized herein are equally guaranteed to male and female indigenous individuals.

RECONNECT

1. Briefly describe three common problems faced by Indigenous peoples.

2. In you view, will the UN be successful in improving the situation of the world's Indigenous peoples? Explain.

The Need for Change

The issues that affect Aboriginal people today all have roots that reach long into the past. The reserve system, the residential school system, and legislation such as the Indian Act all undermined and diminished Aboriginal cultures. Over two centuries of systemic discrimination have taken their toll in Aboriginal communities, evident in higher-than-average rates of unemployment and suicide, and widespread poverty and poor health. Nobody expects these conditions to be reversed quickly. But both Aboriginal and non-Aboriginal people agree that any hope for change depends on Aboriginal peoples gaining more control over their lives, specifically through self-government.

The Royal Commission on Aboriginal Peoples (RCAP) proposed over 400 recommendations to prevent crisis in the future. The focus of these recommendations is on establishing Aboriginal self-government and compensating Aboriginal peoples for the losses they have sustained with land, resources and cash.

Changes in Aboriginal communities will mean changes for all Canadians. If past experience is any guide, Canadians may have trouble accepting some of the changes, especially those requiring the spending of more money. Opinion polls have usually shown, however, that most Canadians favour some form of self-government for Aboriginal peoples. Whether Canadians will be able to accept the kinds of changes suggested by the Royal Commission on Aboriginal Peoples remains to be seen.

The Government's Responsibility

In its 1998 Statement of Reconciliation, the federal government acknowledged that its actions resulted in "the erosion of the political, economic and social systems of Aboriginal people and nations." It formal-

Figure 37-1 Tagak Curley of Nunavut Construction. A former Minister of Energy, Mines and Resources for the Northwest Territories, Curley is involved in the building of the legislature in Iqualuit. It will be the home of the new Nunavut government.

ly expressed its "profound regret" for its past actions. It ends with the following statement:

> Reconciliation is an ongoing process. In renewing our partnership, we must ensure that the mistakes which marked our past relationship are not repeated. The Government of Canada recognizes that policies that sought to assimilate Aboriginal people, women and men, are not the way to build a strong country. We must instead continue to find ways in which Aboriginal people can participate fully in the economic, political, cultural and social life of Canada in a manner which preserves and enhances the collective identities of Aboriginal

communities and allows them to evolve and flourish in the future. Working together to achieve our shared goals will benefit all Canadians, Aboriginal and non-Aboriginal alike.

The document represents a major symbolic shift in the government's approach to Aboriginal people. The statement was accompanied by an Action Plan that includes the establishment of an Independent Land Claims Commission, and commitments to: healing for residential school students; Aboriginal policing; Aboriginal businesses; housing, water and sewage facilities; head-start programs for Aboriginal children; an Aboriginal Health Institute; and stable transfer payments to Aboriginal governments and institutions. The plan, however, does not specify who will administer the $600 million allocated to implementation, nor how the money will be distributed among reserve communities, Métis, and urban Aboriginals. Many feel that the next step is for the government to address the more central rec-

ommendations of the RCAP Report: action on land, resources, and self-government, and the establishment of a House of First Peoples to advise Parliament.

Whatever the future path of Canada's Aboriginal peoples, as the statement noted, "Working together to achieve our shared goals will benefit Canadians, Aboriginal and non-Aboriginal alike."

Figure 37-2 Phanuelie Palluq of Loloolik, N.W.T. performs a drum dance during the ceremony at which Indian Affairs Minister Jane Stewart read the Statement of Reconciliation.

Visions and Voices

"I hope that more youth begin to get in touch with their cultures and traditions."
—D.J. Wemigwans, 19, member of the Ojibwa Nation.

"Our people will not give up or abandon that idea of having our own order of government in Canada."
—Ovide Mercredi, member of the Cree Nation, former national chief of the Assembly of First Nations.

"The vision for the future is of a dual world—one in which both traditional ways and modern are followed, one in which people are equally skilled in the worlds of business and government and of survival on the land....

....It is a vision of a world in which the First Nations people are owners as well as employees, managers as well as users, governors as well as citizens.

The vision for the future is of a world where the First Nations remember that the land and resources are the gift of the Creator, gifts given for the survival of the people, gifts to be used, stewarded and respected."
—Kingfisher Lake First Nation, Wunnumin Lake First Nation, Shibogama Interim Planning Board, *Continuity and Change*, 1997.

RECONNECT

1. Do you personally support the ideas expressed in the excerpt from the Statement of Reconciliation? Explain.

2. Outline your vision of the future of Aboriginal peoples in Canada.

GLOSSARY

alienation   to feel isolated or detached from society or the majority.

alliances   agreements between two or more groups usually formalized by a treaty.

apartheid   a policy introduced in South Africa in 1948 segregating people based on race.

assimilate   to absorb people into a larger social group.

bias   a preference that makes it difficult or impossible to judge fairly.

clans   social and political organizations in Aboriginal societies made up of related groups and families, often sharing a totem or symbol.

coercive   using force to control something.

Cold War   the period between 1945 and 1991 marked by political tension between the United States and the Soviet Union and the threat of war this created.

comprehensive claims   Aboriginal claims for land usually involving the traditional use and occupancy of the land where Aboriginal title has never been settled through treaties.

cultural appropriation   taking elements of another culture and using or presenting it as one's own or with one's own.

cultures   the customs, civilization, and achievements of a particular people or time.

curators   employees of a museum or art gallery who are responsible for the collections.

ecology   the study of plants and animals in relation to each other and their habitats.

ecosystems   communities of plants and animals within certain physical environments.

enfranchisement   to grant the right to vote.

ethnographers   people who study various cultures.

exonerated   cleared of wrongdoing or blame.

genealogies   accounts of lines of descent traced from common ancestors.

holistic   the treatment of the whole person, including mental and social factors, rather than the symptoms of the problem or disease.

Indigenous peoples   peoples whose homelands have been taken over by peoples from other lands.

inherent (inherent right)   an existing right that a person may claim.

matrilineal   a relationship based on kinship with the mother or female line.

mediators   people who intervene between groups or individuals in a dispute in order to help reach an agreement.

patrilineal   a relationship based on kinship with the father or male line.

patrons   people who give financial or other support to a person, cause, work of art, or arts organization.

pemmican   dried meat mixed to a paste with melted fat and berries.

potlatches   celebrations, practised among Aboriginal peoples of the West Coast, at which the hosts present gifts to the guests.

precedents   cases that serve as examples for later cases.

referendum   submitting an issue to the direct vote of the people.

reserves   areas of land set aside for the use of Status Indians.

rituals   a prescribed order of performing rites.

self-sufficiency   the ability to take care of one's needs without depending on someone else.

social history   the history of a society and the relations of people or groups in the society.

sovereign   independent.

sovereignty   the right to self-government.

specific claims   Aboriginal claims for fulfillment of a treaty usually involving land and resources.

stereotype (stereotypical)   an oversimplified and unjustified mental picture of how a particular group of people behaves.

systemic discrimination   widespread and unfair treatment of a particular group of people that is the result of the way an entire system is organized.

title   the legal right to the possession of property.

veto   the power or right to reject or refuse to consent to something.

vision quest   a sacred ceremony among some Aboriginal peoples in which someone goes to a secluded place to fast and communicate with the spiritual world, often through visions.

wards   people placed under the protection of the government.

White Paper   a 1969 government report on Aboriginal peoples.